TOMORROW'S ARCHITECTURAL HERITAGE

TOMORROW'S ARCHITECTURAL HERITAGE

Landscape and Buildings in the Countryside

J.M. FLADMARK , G.Y. MULVAGH *and* B.M. EVANS

FOREWORD BY
HRH The Prince of Wales

MAINSTREAM
PUBLISHING

EDINBURGH AND LONDON

Copyright © The Countryside Commission for Scotland and Gillespies, 1991

First published in Great Britain by
MAINSTREAM PUBLISHING COMPANY (EDINBURGH) LTD
7 Albany Street
Edinburgh EH1 3UG

With support from the Countryside Commission for Scotland

British Library Cataloguing in Publication Data
Fladmark J. M.
    Tomorrow's Architectural Heritage: Landscape and Buildings in the Countryside
    1. Architecture, modern style
    I. Title   II. Mulvagh, G. Y.   III. Evans, B. M.

    ISBN 1-85158-378-5

Book Design by James Hutcheson & Paul Keir, Edinburgh
Typeset in 10/12pt Sabon by Hewer Text Composition Services, Edinburgh
Printed in Great Britain by Butler & Tanner Ltd, Frome, Somerset

ACKNOWLEDGEMENTS

We were overwhelmed by the generous response to our many calls for help, which kept our spirits up in a task that took longer than expected. Without the backing of the Countryside Commission for Scotland and the support of Gillespies, the project simply would not have been possible. We much valued the encouragement from Commissioners, particularly the expert advice from Robert Steedman and Mark Turnbull, and we also record our thanks to three successive Commission Directors. After retirement, John Foster continued to act as our adviser and we have benefitted greatly from his critical judgement based on a lifetime of interest in the subject of countryside design. Michael Taylor is remembered for his support at a time when the project was almost abandoned, and we are indebted to the present Director, Duncan Campbell, who suggested several improvements to the manuscript. Other members of Commission staff who deserve thanks are Alison Grant, Dr Roderick Fairley, Lorne Gill, Alan Stewart and Iain Rennick, whose penmanship in final editing helped to smooth out the wrinkles created by three authors.

We are grateful for the unstinting support given by the partners of Gillespies and their staff, particularly Andrew Follies and Douglas Stonelake. Others who helped at times of need were Bruce Ferguson, Dr Jan Vaage (Agricultural University of Norway), Robert Stewart (Moray District Council) and James MacKinnon (Scottish Office Environment Department).

The process of study for the book went through several phases. A report of the original research work by Gillespies was discussed with local authority councillors and representatives from the landscape and building professions and industry at a series of workshops, the feedback from which provided the basis for the structure and content of the book. Much valuable assistance was received from colleagues at the Scottish Tourist Board, Scottish Enterprise, Highlands and Islands Enterprise, Historic Scotland and the Royal Commission for the Ancient and Historical Monuments of Scotland, especially Ian Gow. Several experts were invited to read an early draft of the text and we record thanks for both constructive criticism and encouragement from Patrick Myhill (Highland Regional Council), David Penman (Perth and Kinross District Council), Dr David Walker (Chief Inspector of Historic Buildings), Charles Prosser (Royal Fine Art Commission for Scotland), Edwina Proudfoot (University of St Andrews), Professor Seaton Baxter (Robert Gordons Institute of Technology) and Dr Brian

Hanson (the Prince and Princess of Wales' Office). Without their considerable help, many of the early shortcomings would have remained, and we are also grateful to those who provided material for Chapter 6 on recent and current practice in Scotland.

Special thanks go to His Royal Highness The Prince of Wales and Charles McKean, whose views on architecture have been a source of much inspiration, and we are grateful to them for writing the Foreword and Introduction. Among those who have helped with the illustrations, we are grateful to Reinhard Behrens and Alan Braby for gracing this book with their fine drawings, and to others who allowed the use of photographs, prints and drawings from their collections, each individually attributed in the text. The encouragement of Bill Campbell and Peter MacKenzie at Mainstream has been much appreciated, and without the steady hand of Penny Clarke we would have found it difficult to reach our goal. The patience of our typists, Anne Bankier, Helen Huxley, Janette McLean and Anne Sweet was also greatly appreciated.

J. M. Fladmark, G. Y. Mulvagh and B. M. Evans
Perth and Glasgow, April 1991

CONTENTS

FOREWORD

By HRH The Prince of Wales

Building in the countryside must be one of the greatest challenges facing an architect. It requires even more of a sensitivity to context than building in towns. It is in the countryside that one experiences true 'timelessness', and so few today have the necessary rapport – that essential empathy with the rural environment – which makes successful buildings possible there.

In Scotland the countryside is of primary importance. How often I have seen badly-designed and insensitive concrete bridges destroy the very 'essence' of their settings – ostensibly to make those places more accessible to the many coming to see them. I would describe such blots on the landscape, in the words of Ruskin, as 'standing with the insolence of a moment amid the majesty of all time'.

Principles such as those contained in this most useful book may help us to comprehend the 'timelessness' of the natural landscape a little more. If some of them seem to be truisms, then that is no bad thing – for much of the problem lies in the obvious, small things we have forgotten, or which have been knocked out of us by professional training of one sort or another. If we are reminded of just a few of these things as we read this book it will have achieved its purpose.

Charles

Kensington Palace

INTRODUCTION

By Charles McKean

If you have any feeling left for this country of Scotland your first reaction to reading this book should be one of rage that such a book as this should be necessary. Your second should be gratitude that the Canutes of the Countryside Commission should have been prepared to stem the remorseless erosion of the Scottish countryside in such a clear and well-illustrated way.

This volume seeks to teach academically what our forefathers learnt through experience and intuition. It reveals the shrewdness with which they located individual buildings and settlements, and how they understood the need to select sites for maximum shelter, water and accessibility. Their buildings were the product of a local response using easily available materials to well-understood living patterns. Above all, they respected the Scottish climate in which wind-driven rain is normally horizontal but, in favourite spots like Iona, even comes upwards.

Clough Williams Ellis first warned of the threat to Britain's character represented by the 'octopus' of ribbon and suburban development almost 70 years ago. In *Building Scotland* published 50 years ago, Robert Hurd and Alan Reiach applied that warning to Scotland. The need for this new book is a measure of the extent to which those previous warnings have gone unheeded, as Scotland's identity has been sacrificed for short-term gain.

In 1930 John Buchan warned Parliament that in his view the time was not far off when Scotland would have nothing distinctive left to show the world. One purpose of this volume is to indicate (to those suffering from cultural amnesia) some elements of that distinctiveness: what, in short, makes Scotland Scottish. The Scottish identity is as inherent from its landscape and vegetation as it is from its building. Ash, hazel, birch, alder, rowan and oak comprise a Scots wood. Oak being scarce (all the oak trees in Fife were used in building a single galleon, the *Great Michael*, in 1511), you would be correct in assuming that Scotland was not a country of timber buildings since none of the other trees provide the requisite long-span beams. Consequently, until cheap long-span timber became available from the Baltic in the early 18th century, Scotland's architectural identity was governed by the width of a stone vault.

Architecture, wrote Sir Banister Fletcher, is governed by the same factors throughout the world and it is how they differ from region to region that creates architectural identity. They include geology, geography, climate, religion, politics and economy – of which the effects of economy are most apparent in building. Who built, what they built, and how well they built it, is social history in stone. Dressed stone, being expensive in Scotland if masons had to be shipped from the east, was a sign of wealth: harling or lime wash over rubble (in part or in whole) was a simple way of concealing its absence. Thus grew a spare architectural tradition of dressed or carved stone carefully applied against a smooth but usually coloured or white background. This formed the aesthetic of the Scottish Renaissance.

This book correctly emphasises the importance of colour to this country. The light is weak and the sun only occasional, and buildings should respond to and enhance light, not absorb it. To judge by some recent buildings – particularly the advent of the 'cow-pat School of Architecture' (low buildings with a large brown roof, low brown walls and brown stained windows) – we seem to have forgotten Scotland's intense colouring so vividly expressed in the paintings of Sir D. Y. Cameron.

The threat to Scotland's character is the consequence of social change, of which the most significant is transport. First shipping, then rail, then road opened rural Scotland to cheaper, non-local materials whose advent priced local materials out of business. The more remote the site, the more the putative economic benefit of a prefabricated import. The advent of new materials, in itself, need not be deleterious. Corrugated iron, for example, has been used for nigh on 200 years in rural Scotland, and has become an accepted part of the scene. Cast-iron prefabrication became common 150 years ago, since when it has become equally assimilated. What matters is that it *fits*. The issue, therefore, is less the materials themselves so much as the skill and sensitivity with which they are deployed. The kit timber house, for example, is simply a prefabricated frame, and in the 19th century we transformed iron and steel frames to produce highly characteristic Scottish buildings. If it is true that, as the authors suggest, only traditional materials should be used beside existing buildings, it is a sad commentary on the state of contemporary design in Scotland. Northern Italy or Norway, for example which still retain their intuitive flair and national identity, have demonstrated amply the magnificent potential of contemporary design and contemporary materials as a graceful complement to historic structures. What jars is the sight of a kit house with a hacienda façade of thin granite sheets erupting like a carbuncle upon an otherwise innocent Scottish hillside. Moreover, irrespective of their individual design, humble or fashionable alike, their environs are overwhelmed by the impact of roads, pavements, access driveways and garages — the appalling paraphernalia which has turned beleaguered communities throughout rural Scotland into scenes reminiscent of the Wild West, with all the shanty town impact of Dodge City.

The authors recommend that new buildings are constructed either as natural extensions to older settlements, or entirely separate. They understand the advertisement-led desire for a dream house in the country, but explain how that desire is unattainable for the mass of the population without killing the countryside. That desire, in any case, is corrupted to a surrogate version in the speculative suburb as we practise it today. The day when Scotland can achieve a suburban layout appropriate to the country's character is much to be desired.

There are some pitfalls in seeking inspiration solely in history, as the respective careers of Sir Robert Lorimer and Charles Mackintosh reveal. Lorimer went back into the past and, for the most part, stayed there, boasting of the House of Formakin that it was the best 17th-century building that he had done. Mackintosh was also inspired by the 17th century, but he abstracted from its design to produce a contemporary architecture he regarded as both truly Scottish and modern. It was thus Mackintosh and not Lorimer who became the primary inspiration for succeeding generations. The lesson is salutary if we are to avoid architectural myth – chiefly from those who have the laudable aim to be Scottish without understanding that the culture has developed since the 17th century. In response to accusations that his film *Brigadoon* was a travesty of Scotland, the producer Arthur Freed responded: 'I went to Scotland and found nothing there that looks like Scotland' – so he faked it up.

The urgent necessity for a book such as this is caused by the combination of cultural deracination, a loss of intuition and a morbid eagerness to devalue architecture and design. The difficulty of assimilating social change is exacerbated by the fundamental problem of poor design. Those who see land and construction solely as another business should find this book invaluable, for if they follow its guidance they will avoid justified obloquy. It should act as a knuckle between visually-illiterate amnesiacs, who need to be told what to do on the one hand, and as a guidance for the creative on the other. To paraphrase Mrs Beaton, if you plan to build in the countryside, first find your architect; second, ensure that he/she has the intuitive understanding of designing in the Scottish countryside implicit in this book; and lastly, provide a copy as a good *aide-memoire*. For anybody else, it should be compulsory reading.

Eildon Hill North, showing
dwelling platforms of the
settlement that existed
about the time when the
Romans invaded Scotland
(© *Historic Scotland*)

Entrance to Totaig Broch on
the south side of Loch Duich
– an example of stone
detailing from the Iron Age
(left). Cleit on St Kilda – the
island-equivalent of the field
barn used for the storage of
peat, hay and produce – an
ancient building type
designed in response to
climate, the other gable
being dome-shaped to divert
the ferocious gales (right)

CHAPTER ONE

RESPECTING OUR HERITAGE

To gain an historical perspective of our architectural heritage it is necessary to understand the factors which have shaped our natural and built environment – factors which together make up the cultural landscape of Scotland. Its basic structure is derived from geological processes, and its appearance from the nature and extent of vegetation and ground cover and from man's habitation and cultivation, all of which are also influenced by climate. Taken together these factors give landscapes their character and sense of place, and the following pages describe the different landscape types to be found in Scotland as well as man's impact on them, and then trace the development of building styles through from Neolithic times to the present day.

THE NATURAL ENVIRONMENT

Scotland is not a country of simple rules and easy solutions when it comes to dealing with the landscape setting of buildings. Within its land area and fringe of offshore islands can be found a great diversity of landforms and habitats. The geological forces that gave shape to the land have left a large mountain range north of the Highland Boundary Fault, known as the Grampians, and another south of the Southern Upland Fault, which for geological and climatic reasons consists of more rounded hills. In between these upland areas lie the Central Lowlands, a belt of low-lying land that is now the most densely inhabited part of Scotland. It varies in character from coastal to inland and from flat to hilly, but it represents a general type of landscape that is open and wide with gently sweeping lines spanning a low horizon (see p 41). This central plain is bordered by glens and straths. In the north are the Perthshire and Angus glens which penetrate the Grampians and in the south, the Border valleys of the rolling Southern Uplands, both of which are characterised by a sense of enclosure and high horizons.

The seaboard of the west and north-west is deeply indented by lochs and glens, flanked by dramatic mountain scenery. The Great Glen Fault forms a deep trough-like dissection of the northern mainland with whale-back mountains on either side. The glens of the Western Highlands are different in character from those in Perthshire and Angus. Rather than being wide and rounded, many are often deep, narrow and angular, while the combination of land and water gives the coastal and island landscapes of the far north-west a special character, further enhanced by dramatic mountain scenery. The sea lochs could be regarded as valley landscapes, but the presence of a wide body of water reduces the sense of enclosure, and there are long vistas up, down and across the lochs.

The retreating glaciers of the last Ice Age revealed the varied landform described above, and material gouged from the hills spread over the valley floors and coastal plains to form knolls and terraces. As the last glaciers and snowfields in the higher hills receded, vegetation such as dwarf birch, willow, juniper and sedges took over. The climate warmed and by 8000 BC the birch had arrived. Seeds dispersed by the wind ensured this pioneering species spread rapidly, and birch forests quickly shaded out much of the earlier juniper. Hazel followed closely on its heels and this early woodland habitat, together with continued climatic amelioration, allowed mixed deciduous forests of rowan, ash, oak and elm to become established in parts of south and west Scotland by 7000 BC. By this time the yew, an early arrival, had been joined by another evergreen, the Scots pine, which gradually invaded the birch and hazel forests of the north and east and thus began the Old Caledonian Forest, not a pure pine forest but one with a strong mixture of deciduous trees.

Vestiges of these early forests still remain, as in the Speyside forests of Abernethy and Rothiemurchus. In the extreme north of the mainland and in parts of the Hebrides and Orkney, the birch and hazel forests remained dominant, with some aspen and alder but very little pine and oak. Shetland and many of the Hebridean islands, on the other hand, never supported a full forest cover, and dwarf shrub heaths have prevailed there since the end of the last Ice Age.

By 6000 BC much of Scotland had a landscape of richly varied forest cover and it was at this time, when the forest was at its greatest extent, that two things happened. Britain was severed from mainland Europe by the formation of the English Channel, hence slowing new plant colonisation. At the same time, people began to extend their colonisation of the country, at first hunting and fishing along the coast, but gradually moving inland. It was this movement which had the single most important effect on the appearance of our landscape.

THE LANDSCAPE OF MAN

What follows is inspired by Geoffrey and Susan Jellicoe's book *The Landscape of Man*, written in 1975, in which they set themselves the task of describing how the environment has been shaped by man right from historic times up until the present day. In Scotland this process started with the first Neolithic farmers, who cleared the light upland and coastal soils for agricultural and pastoral use. Remains of settlements and burials show that colonisation accelerated in the Bronze Age and better tools enabled improved building techniques and methods of cultivation, so that by the early Iron Age the land had been widely cleared and supported an increased population. Over a period of about 3,000 years the native vegetation of Scotland was thereby gradually transformed from predominantly forest cover to more open land and this, together with the cool, wet weather of a maritime climate, led to the development of boggy moors and heathland, with the growth of peat being so extensive that it spread over much land previously farmed.

Descriptions of southern Scotland by the Romans support evidence that upland areas were by then mainly bare, only valley floors and steep slopes still having any forest cover. After the Roman withdrawal the Celtic peoples continued the expansion of settlement and farming. The Vikings and the Normans added further pressure on the land and intensified the demand for timber – this indeed, became so scarce in the 13th and 14th centuries that legislation was enacted to prohibit fires and restrict grazing and the cutting of oak. In spite of this, the original oak forests were almost completely exhausted. Indeed, there are now very few sites where truly ancient trees can be seen, examples being in the Great Wood of Cawdor, the Cadzow Oaks in Hamilton High Park (see p 35) and the Birnam Oaks,

Neolithic timber hall dating from about 3500 BC at Balbridie on Deeside, based on excavations by Dr Ian Ralston and Nicholas Reynolds in 1977–8 *(Drawing: Alan Braby, © I. Ralston)*

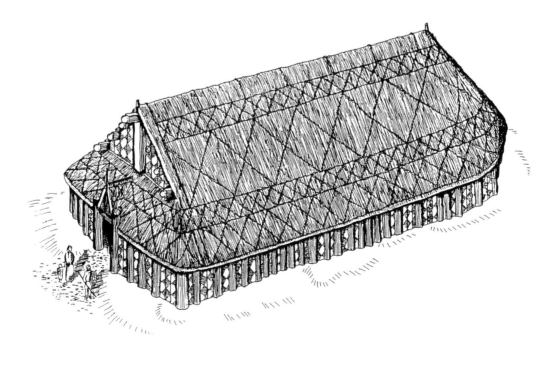

although almost all ancient woodland in Scotland has been modified to some extent through the activities of man.

With little lowland forest left, timber supplies were sought elsewhere. Iron works and salt pans led the demand and, during the two centuries preceding the Industrial Revolution, charcoal burning for these and other purposes had a devastating effect on the remaining forests of the north and west. Many sites of platforms for charcoal burning are known, and there are still remains of several local iron furnaces. Although some attempts were made to introduce positive woodland management on the Highland estates after the Jacobite rising in 1745, for another 150 years exploitation continued to satisfy the demands of a society increasingly based on industrial and commercial activity.

The agricultural improvements that began in the middle of the 18th century affected the Highlands and the Lowlands differently. Sheep were introduced to the Highlands in large numbers and their grazing inhibited the regeneration of the forests. The popularity of acquiring Highland estates for sporting purposes, which continues to this day, allowed a large increase in red deer herds and has also added greatly to the difficulties of forest recovery. This combination of sheep and sport motivated certain landowners to clear people from the land so that large parts of the Highlands are now without human habitation.

In the Lowlands the land was enclosed and drained for crops and dairy farming. The larger holdings associated with grand country houses were surrounded by formal gardens and extensive landscaped grounds, and the planting of ornamental woods, shelterbelts and hedgerows created a varied landscape of open fields and woodland enclosure. However, in recent years this heritage of intimate field patterns has been destroyed in some areas by the uprooting of hedgerows and removal of dykes to allow the more convenient use of modern machinery. Equally serious has been the failure to maintain those traditional features which remain.

THE IMPRINT OF BUILDINGS

Climate has been the single most important factor governing the way buildings have been sited, shaped and constructed. Over the long periods of time described above, there have been fluctuations in temperature. In the late Iron Age the weather was relatively mild, while during the Middle Ages the temperature dropped to give long winters and a need for more robust shelter. What makes Britain so very different from many other European countries is its offshore position. Exposure to an unpredictable maritime climate, with high rainfall and strong winds, has meant that, when the need for a defensive position has not been paramount, the native people have for the most part chosen sheltered locations to live in, building their dwellings

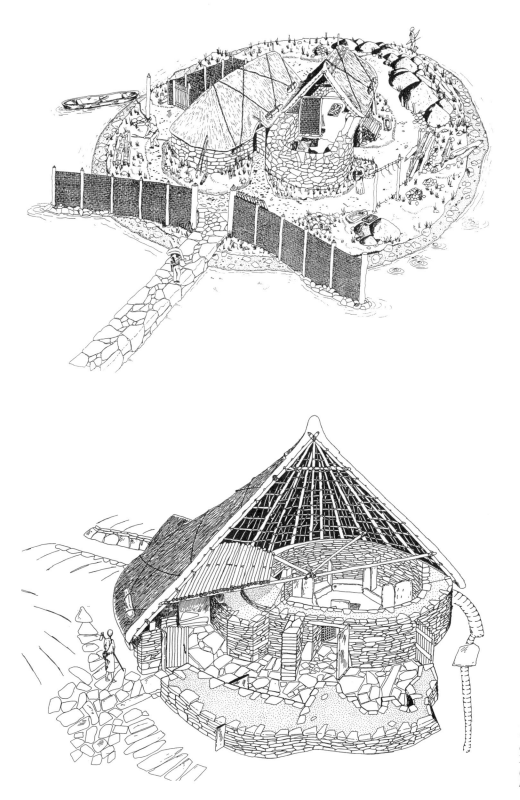

Neolithic island settlement at Loch Olabhat on North Uist, based on excavations currently in progress by Dr Ian Armit *(Drawing: Alan Braby)*

Early Iron Age roundhouse at Toftsness on Sanday in Orkney, based on excavations by Steve Dockrill in 1985–8 *(Drawing: Alan Braby, © Historic Scotland)*

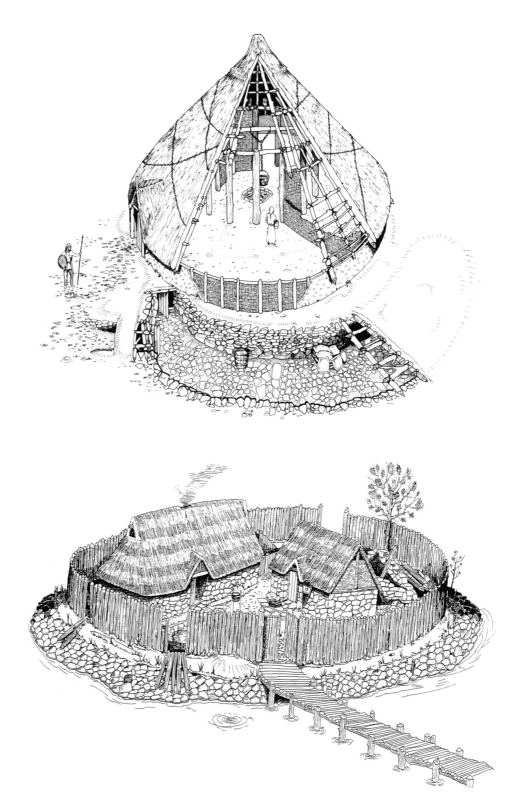

Iron Age roundhouse with souterrain, based on excavations at Newmill in Perthshire by Dr Trevor Watkins in 1980, being contemporary with the Eildon Hill township and similar to the houses found there *(Drawing: Alan Braby)*

Medieval crannog on fictitious site *(Drawing: Alan Braby)*

with pitched roofs to cope with the elements.

When the Neolithic people of Scotland moved inland to start clearing the land for agriculture, they erected houses with walls of wattle from pliable hazel. These were either rectangular or round, often with stone or turf foundations, and finished with daub or clay to keep out rain and snow. In the islands and in exposed coastal areas, where few trees were to hand, they made use of the abundant supply of stone. Therefore, from early times the style of building has varied according to local conditions and availability of materials. Archaeological evidence shows that as long ago as 3000 BC stone houses were erected with fitted furniture of beds, benches and cupboards, examples surviving at Knap of Howe and Skara Brae in Orkney, and Stanydale and Jarlshof in Shetland.

Some of the early settlers had an amazing ability to handle enormous blocks of stone (the megalithic tradition). Others used dry masonry and corbelling techniques with considerable skill, and the survival of so many chambered tombs speaks for the quality of their work. Indeed, the many stone circles and sites of standing stones from this time provide further evidence of their building and engineering skills.

There is less evidence of timber structures, however, as nothing remains above ground to tell us about them. Nevertheless, post-holes found at some excavations confirm that both timber circles and timber buildings existed. Much is still being learned about these, and the recent excavation by Ian Ralston of a timber hall at Balbridie on Deeside has caused the history of early timber architecture to be reassessed. Rather than being from Anglo Saxon times as originally thought, carbon dating has now shown that this building dates from about 3500 BC and it probably had a thatched roof at an angle of 45 degrees on a rectangular floor plan which measured 27x13m (see p 17). The technique of construction was well in advance of contemporary practice elsewhere in Europe, the roof being carried on two widely spaced rows of posts to form a central aisle entirely free of structural members. The outer walls were formed by hefty square timbers rammed into the ground and the roof had a ridge beam of massive dimensions. A similar house has been excavated at Balfarg in Fife, and these two examples confirm the early antecedence of rectangular timber buildings in Scotland.

When the Romans came, they found a civilisation with a distinct architecture. The Celtic people had arrived from Europe about a thousand years earlier, bringing with them the technology of iron-making, and their enduring imprint on our landscape was to introduce a different stone-building tradition – one that has survived into this century. The most remarkable and uniquely Scottish of all was the broch settlement. The imposing defensive structure of the broch itself was surrounded by a village of houses and walled enclosures – the settlement at Gurness in Orkney being one of the best examples to survive relatively intact (see pp 36–7).

They were mainly found in the north and west of the mainland and on the islands, while a smaller version of the broch, the dun, served as a focus for small agricultural communities and had a similar geographic distribution. The houses were also round, sometimes set into the ground like at Valtos on Lewis, or above ground as at Toftsness on Sanday in Orkney (see p 19, bottom).

In east and south Scotland society was organised around hilltop settlements. Although often described as hill forts due to their defensive enclosures, they appear to have been well-organised townships. Their size varied and the largest were tribal strongholds, such as Traprain in East Lothian and Eildon Hill North near Melrose (see p 14, top). Some 300 circular foundations survive on Eildon North, representing remains of a substantial settlement. There were many others, Edinburgh and Stirling having started in this way, and those at Dunadd (Argyll), Alcluith (Dunbarton) and Dunsinane (Perthshire) were also important in the early history of the Scottish nation. These were the focal points in a hierarchical settlement structure, each unit providing functional space for living and storage, as well as enclosure for growing crops and holding livestock.

The brochs and the hill townships were linked to a system of small agricultural settlements. Some were clusters of houses with defensive enclosures, others were small groups or individual dwellings. The houses were mostly round, with low walls of stone or timber (see p 20, top). Associated with these was the souterrain, a curved underground passage with masonry walls and a roof of long stone slabs or, in some cases, a low pitched roof of timber. Once thought to have been used for refuge in times of strife, they are now recognised as having been for storage, like our modern cellars, with entrances from both inside and outside the house. Similarly, crannogs were also common at the time, round or rectangular houses set on artificially created islands in lochs, a narrow causeway or bridge providing access from the shore (see p 20, bottom).

After the collapse of the Roman occupation there is little evidence to suggest that their style of design and building techniques had a lasting impact. Any stone structures were subsequently used by the natives as quarries for their own projects. The military camps were dismantled, but the remains of the Antonine Wall left a significant landscape feature across central Scotland. Some of the hilltop settlements were reoccupied, and people in the north and west continued to live in their brochs and duns for another century, adapting and rebuilding to cope with changing circumstances. However, as the defensive structures became redundant, so they in turn became convenient quarries for less imposing dwellings and some of the broch villages expanded into sizeable communities. The crannogs continued in use, and some medieval tower houses were built on such island sites.

The architecture of the early Christian era was a mixture of round and

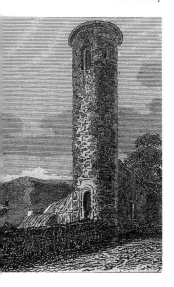

The round tower of Abernethy

rectangular buildings, the main generic types from early times. Construction was generally of either stone or timber, or a combination of both. It is believed that the buildings of the early Christian missionaries, St Ninian at Whithorn and St Columba on Iona, were made of timber, but there were many chapels and churches built in stone and clay, and the surviving examples of round towers built by the Culdees, at Brechin and Abernethy, bear witness to fine masonry techniques. The rectangular 'black' house of the Western Isles (see p 38, top) had stone outer walls, but many buildings were also made of turf, both types continuing in use until the end of the last century.

The Vikings in the north and then the Normans in the south brought Scotland within the mainstream of European influence, the latter being more significant. Many churches and abbeys were founded, heralding a new era of architecture, and monasteries introduced horticulture, better farming methods and new livestock. This had profound consequences for the countryside as did the new feudal system, which was administered from motte and bailey castles. The Normans also introduced a large number of new burghs to promote commerce, trade and craft. Although the plan for these burghs varied, the street and market-place were normally laid out on an axis related to the castle, abbey or church. The distinction between private and public open space was clearly defined, and the boundary of each property was marked out by stockades or stone walls, as was the perimeter of the whole settlement. In the countryside the stronghold of the laird was the tower house (see p 39, bottom), with auxiliary buildings enclosed by the barmkin wall. The ordinary people who worked the land lived in small communities, each of a few families, which became known as 'clachans' in the Highlands and 'fermtouns' in the Lowlands.

The Scottish Renaissance (1500–1650) was a period of significant change with many lasting effects. New burghs were introduced and many of the existing burghs were replanned. Timber and turf houses were replaced by stone buildings, and thatch gave way to slate, fired-clay tiles and stone slabs. The typical burgh house of this period had a ground floor that was often vaulted and used for storage, kitchens and sometimes livestock. Living space was on the first floor and reached by an outside stairway – good examples of this type are to be seen in Culross. Farmers lived in similar bastel-type houses, and recent evidence suggests that these were more numerous in the countryside than was once thought.

An interest in the art of gardening was a trend set by Scottish kings, who had strong connections with the French court where the formal Italian renaissance garden was in vogue. New gardens with parterres, topiary, avenues, terraces and statuary were established to provide a new setting for royal palaces. The example was followed by the nobility at their country seats and, on a smaller scale, by prosperous farmers and merchants in the burghs. The use of timber palisades around properties was replaced by

The old manse at Howford Bridge, Nairn, showing a turf-built dwelling, part rendered and limewashed, a type of building that survived in use throughout the countryside into this century (© I. Rae)

stone boundary walls, which also made it easier to form terraces on sloping ground. Gardens were designed for pleasure as well as utility, and were planned as an outdoor extension to built living space. This concept, treating the garden as the external aspect of architecture, is well exemplified in many later illustrations (see pp 122–3), but the most enduring testament to the close alliance between architect and gardener at this time was John Reid's book *The Scots Gardener*. First published in 1683, it has so far run into six editions with the latest in 1988, which speaks for its lasting relevance.

The agricultural changes that started in the 18th century introduced the landscape pattern we see today. The rural subsistence economy, based on runrig farming and centred on family groups, was swept away by owners intent on farming in their own right. They drained the land, created a new field system, and introduced new methods of cultivation and husbandry. Some owners employed architects to design houses in the classical manner, surrounding them with ornamental and kitchen gardens that were set in landscapes designed to relate to the new field pattern. Farm steadings were planned around a courtyard, frequently designed with a symmetrical façade in the Palladian manner. Cottages for farm workers were usually well separated from the main house and laid out in south-facing rows with their own garden plots. Owners of large holdings often used the same architect to impose a consistent style throughout an estate, and this gave a unity of appearance in certain areas that has now become part of local tradition.

The shedding of farm labour and the growth in rural industries led to another important new trend in the 19th century, the planning and development of new villages. The main lesson from these lies in the control of layout and built form. This was achieved by simple rules which governed the street layout, the size of plot, the position of the building relative to the street, the height of buildings and use of materials. Indeed, the Industrial Revolution was not entirely confined to the towns and, for economic reasons, many industries found their way into the countryside. Some social reformers even sought to take the industrial worker to the countryside for a better life, like Robert Owen (1771–1858) at New Lanark. The Victorian liking for grandeur meant that industrial buildings were often dressed up to pretend that they were something else. Main façades were often clad in fine masonry and designed on classical lines, and the landscape setting was laid out to give the impression of a palatial residence. The result was to create a built environment in harmony with its surroundings and in tune with the culture of the countryside. The model of farm buildings was sometimes followed, a good example from 1868 being the Cardy Works in Lower Largo (see p 40, bottom).

The advent of the railways also had many significant consequences for the appearance of the countryside, not the least of which was the spread of railway architecture to remote areas (see p 28). Towns expanded and the first commuter settlements began to appear, while those who could afford it

OPPOSITE
George Stewart's plan of 1789 for Bruar shooting lodge on the Atholl Estate. The accommodation is enclosed by a perimeter wall to form a courtyard on the pattern of a farm house from Greek and Roman antiquity (© *His Grace the Duke of Atholl*)

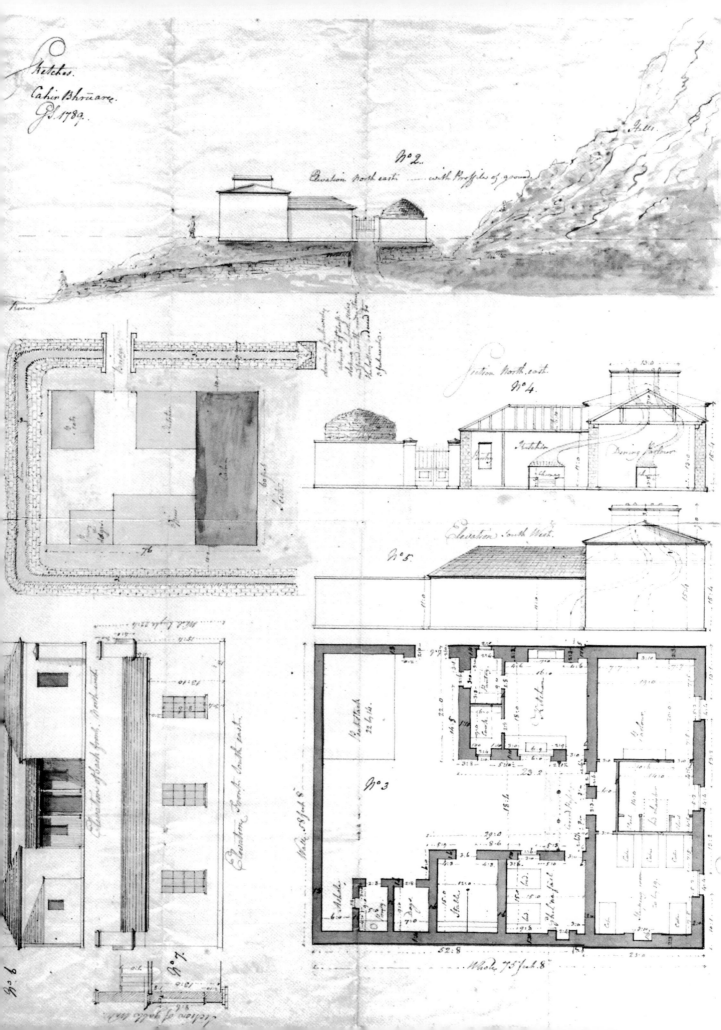

Sketches.
Cahir Bhruare.
GS. 1789.

No 2.
Elevation north east ..... with Profiles of ground.

Section North east.
No 4.

Kitchen   Dining Parlour

Elevation south West.
No 5.

No 3

Elevation of back front, North west.

Elevation Front, South west.

No 7.

W ✦ E

Explaination of ye Court of Offices

A .	The Barn 70 by 16 feet	
B .	Elevation of gabel of do.	
C.C.	The Cart Shades 36½ feet	
D .	The Granary above do.	
E .	Elevation of Shades & granary	
F.F.	Byre & Loft 16 by 12 feet	
G .	Elevation of do.	
H .	Passage from Court to road 12 feet	
	Oversers Room above the Gateway commanding the whole farm	
U.U.	Passages at each side of the Court 12 feet wide	
W .	Passage at the back part of the Court opposite gateway 4 feet	
N:B	Within the board a Stair to the Granary in which is a Trap door for loading the Victual into the Cart Shades	
L.L.	Byre & Loft 24 by 16 feet
N .	Poultry house 12½ by 16
O .	Pigeon house do. do
W.P.	Elevation of Byre, Poultry & Pigeon house
Q.Q.	Straw house 22 by 14 feet
R .	Farm Lads house 16 by 18
S .	Stable 54 feet by 16 feet
T .	Elevation of the Stable gabel

At each side of the entry is a Stair for the oversers room & Lofts for the farm Lads house a Stair & Stair for the garret Stable Loft

In the Elevation of the whole the Walls are intended 9 feet high the Room above the Gateway excepted which is proposed 16 feet

X. a Necessary the front opposite the gateway being an entry to Dung Court

Explanation of Farm house

A .	Family Room 16 by 14 feet
B .	Bed Room 15 by 12 feet
C .	Bed Closett 6½ feet Square
D .	Pantry 6½ by 5½ feet
E .	Small place for garden Utensils
F .	The Necessary 5 by 4 feet

Explaination of Farm house

G .	Kitchen 15 by 12 feet
H .	Milk house 8½ by 6½ feet
J .	Coal house 12 by 5 feet
K .	Small Court inclosed
L .	Elevation of the house
m.m.	proper places for cattle or swine feeding if wanted

5 10 20 30 40 50 60 70 80 90 100 feet Scale

D2

built country houses. The increased ability of people to go on holiday meant new hotels and boarding-houses in parts previously untouched by urban pressures, and since that time it has been less easy to distinguish between urban built form and a truly rural tradition of design.

Landowners tended to use the same architect for their country properties as for their town houses, and the great architects of the 18th and 19th centuries showed great versatility by working with equal competence in urban and rural situations, the combined skills of both garden and building design being their great contribution to our cultural heritage. Notable architect-gardeners were Sir William Bruce (1630–1710) and William Adam (1689–1748), the latter followed by his sons Robert and James. This attachment to the landscaped setting of a building was so strong, in the case of William Adam, that it is said he continued as gardener long after architectural work had been completed at several properties.

A long list of distinguished Scottish designers carried this tradition into the last century, working in a variety of styles that included Scottish baronial, the baroque and classical revivalism. Well-known architects from this period, whose works are worth further study, include William Burn, Thomas Brown, William Henry Playfair, David Hamilton, James Gillespie Graham, Thomas Hamilton, David Bryce, Sir George Gilbert Scott and Sir Robert Rowan Anderson, who in 1892 formed the School of Applied Art in Edinburgh and was a prime mover in 1916 in the establishment of an institute, which later became The Royal Incorporation of Architects in Scotland.

In a class of his own was Alexander 'Greek' Thomson (1817–75) who left a legacy of remarkable buildings. In *Scotstyle*, Fiona Sinclair says of him that he 'far surpassed those [designs] of any of his immediate contemporaries, so wholly original was his interpretation of Greek and Egyptian forms'. His achievements were all the more remarkable since it is said that he never left Scotland but for a single trip to London and occasional visits to friends in Yorkshire. The fact that his knowledge of European architecture was entirely acquired from books may in part account for his unique translation of classicism into 19th-century Scotland. Although best known for his urban buildings set in Glasgow, he also designed many country villas, like Holmwood at Cathcart in Renfrewshire (see pp 30–31), showing his careful handling of the fit between a building and its landscape setting. However, like his contemporaries, he was essentially backward-looking and sought his inspiration from past styles – the postscript to his career being the Alexander Thomson Travelling Studentship to be awarded for the best design in the Greek style. A significant connection in the sea change of ideas, between the old and the new guard at the turn of the century, was the receipt by Charles Rennie Mackintosh of the Alexander Thomson Studentship in 1890.

OPPOSITE
Fully enclosed courtyard steading designed for the Atholl Estate in the 18th century (© *His Grace the Duke of Atholl*)

TOWARDS A NEW HERITAGE

Seen against this rich background of tradition, the question must be asked whether our present contribution has sufficient intrinsic merit to become part of tomorrow's heritage. To understand the way things are done today it is necessary to look back to the 1920s, when a new approach to architecture and design began to emerge that has become known as the Modern Movement. It was a response to the machine-age of the 20th century that sought a new and different expression of function and structure, seeing little relevance in classical form and ornamentation. Its cradle was the Bauhaus School in the German town of Weimar, founded in 1919 by the architect and educationalist Walter Gropius (1883–1963), and from there it spread to the rest of Europe and to North America at the onset of World War II. This movement was driven by an idea that modern architecture transcends national boundaries; it sought to emphasise internationalism and played down styles of regional origin. However, an alternative faction of 'regionalist' architects continued to uphold the principle of local identity and style, and this has grown in membership and fortune in recent years. One such regionalist, Richard England, has observed that the problem with the Modern Movement is that 'it tried to find the universal solution to what was never a universal problem'.

Alongside this modernist approach, discussed more fully in Chapter 6, there are many specific factors that govern current practice. Foremost among these is the car, which has become a dominant element that demands space for access, garaging and parking. Similarly, modern machinery makes earth moving practical on a scale and at a speed not possible with manual methods, which makes site preparation and road building easy, but it does become tempting to ignore natural landform. The high cost of site construction has led to more components being made on the factory floor, leading to the production of components and materials which pay no regard to locality, and the production of complete building-kits is now a common practice. The result is a sameness in appearance that ignores local conditions and customs.

Inappropriate design and use of modern building materials have had an adverse impact on many old settlements. New standards of insulation and glazing techniques have improved living comforts throughout the year, but they have also made it possible to ignore the local climate by erecting buildings in exposed locations where they can be visually intrusive. A serious problem is also the lack of understanding of how to alter old buildings to meet modern requirements, as is discussed in more detail in subsequent chapters.

When making comparisons with the past there are two main differences. One is that the design of a building today will often be treated as a separate exercise from the design of its surroundings. Only after the

Golspie railway station, terminus of the Sutherland railway built in 1868 (© *Highlands & Islands Enterprise*)

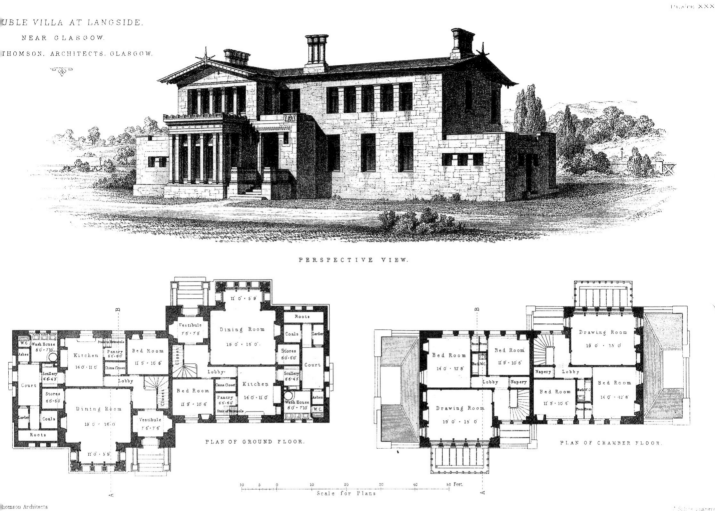

PLATE XXX

UBLE VILLA AT LANGSIDE.

NEAR GLASGOW.

THOMSON, ARCHITECTS, GLASGOW.

PERSPECTIVE VIEW.

PLAN OF GROUND FLOOR.

PLAN OF CHAMBER FLOOR.

Scale for Plans

Thomson Architects

BLACKIE & SON, GLASGOW EDINBURGH & LONDON

building has been completed will work start on the landscape design. Indeed, it is often the case that rural buildings and their landscape settings, unlike their urban counterparts, are not professionally designed at all. The second point is that Scotland's great variety of architectural styles is increasingly ignored. The sameness of kit building is the main culprit, and the flexibility of kit manufacture needs to be more widely understood and applied, along with a greater effort to integrate buildings with their landscape setting.

The following chapters outline principles of good practice. They are not hard and fast rules of design but seek to develop an understanding of the subtle interplay between architecture and landscape. Architects of the past who followed these principles designed buildings that were as pleasing to the eye as their surroundings. The aim should be the same today if we are to create a new built heritage worthy of tomorrow.

The work of Alexander 'Greek' Thomson is internationally admired, his countryside villas being no exception

The double villa at Langside was set on a flat site with few shrubs and trees, the garden treatment being open with lawns sweeping up to the walls (© *RCAHMS*)

29

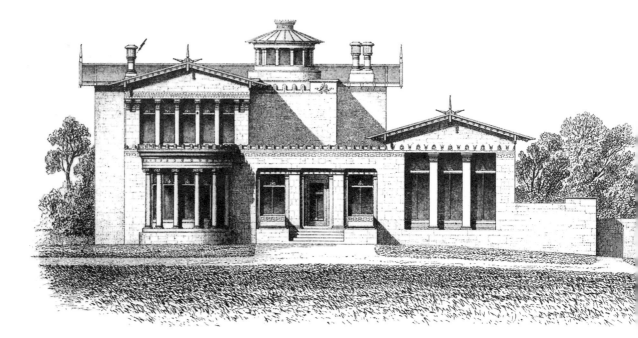

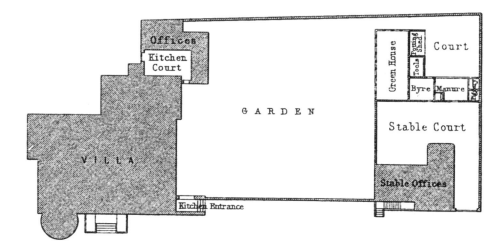

Offices

Kitchen Court

Green House

Tools

Potting Shed

Court

Byre

Manure

VILLA

G A R D E N

Stable Court

Stable Offices

Kitchen Entrance

Holmwood (1958) was set
on a sloping site in a bend of
the River Cart. A fully
enclosed inner courtyard
garden was formed by the
walls between the villa and
the stable offices, all set in
landscaped grounds with
adjusted levels to form the
entrance road and terraces
so that the whole complex
fits into its site *(© RCAHMS)*

RESPECTING OUR HERITAGE

1. The natural environment and man's imprint on it have together produced the countryside that is our cultural landscape.

2. Landform and climate have been the most important natural factors governing the pattern of human habitation.

3. The basic architectural form of buildings has been the same for a remarkably long time.

4. The detailed design of buildings has varied according to the local climate, site conditions, materials, skills and tradition.

5. Imported ideas and styles have stimulated change, but they have been adapted and given the stamp of local tradition according to local needs and the availability of materials.

6. Since the Renaissance, gardens and landscapes have been treated as an integral part of architectural design.

7. Changes in farming practices and the revival of classicism in the 18th century produced an architecture that is still relevant.

8. The rules of design and planning control for new village development in the 19th century were simple but effective.

9. The car and modern building technology have affected our existing heritage and will influence the shape of things to come.

10. Creating an appropriate built heritage for the future will require a greater awareness of, and respect for, the design principles of the past.

OPPOSITE
The Great Glen *(Photo: Patricia and Angus Macdonald)*

Strathardle in Perthshire,
just north of the Highland
Boundary Fault *(Photo:
Lorne Gill)*

The Cadzow Oaks in
Hamilton High Park,
shrouded in the mist of a
history that goes back more
than 600 years (© *Hamilton
District Council*)

The Fortingall Yew, with a
measured girth of 56½ft in
1796, is believed to be more
than 3,000 years old (*Photo:
T. A. Wain, Perth & Kinross
District Council*)

The 'high' street leading to the entrance of the broch *(© Highlands & Islands Enterprise)*

The Broch of Gurness in Orkney, showing late Iron Age settlement arranged along a main street leading to the broch entrance *(Photo: Patricia and Angus Macdonald)*

The blackhouse of the Western Isles has evolved over many centuries. Its walls were not much higher than the surrounding boundary walls, built with the same local stone so that the building merged into the pattern of the landscape, as above at Locheport on North Uist (© *Scottish Tourist Board*). In more recent times they have often received, along with other improvements, a coat of whitewash as below, being the evolutionary link to the modern 'white' house. (*Photo: John W. Mackay*)

Crail in Fife, which received
its Royal Charter in 1310,
still retains the basic layout
typical of many early burghs
*(Photo: Patricia and Angus
Macdonald)*

Loch Leven Castle at
Kinross is one of the best
preserved examples of an
early Scottish towerhouse
with a barmkin wall to
provide security and shelter
*(Photo: Patricia and Angus
Macdonald)*

The planned village of
Gavinton in East Lothian
*(Photo: Patricia and Angus
Macdonald)*

Cardy works in Lower
Largo, Fife, built in 1868 for
the manufacture of fishing
nets, the contemporary
advertising poster showing a
well-integrated layout of
factory, cottage and owner's
residence arranged around a
walled and landscaped
courtyard

Stenton in East Lothian, showing successive phases of development, each respecting the established character of the settlement, with the surrounding countryside remaining free of development other than farm buildings *(Photo: Patricia and Angus Macdonald)*

Steading, house and cottages at Luggate Farm in East Lothian *(Photo: Patricia and Angus Macdonald)*

Like society, architecture has to observe a certain code of good manners to be successful – the tightly-knit urban fabric and attractive roofscape of Gardenstown on the Buchan coast are the product of adhering to the basic rules of design laid down when it was established as a planned settlement in 1720 *(Photo: Dennis Hardley)*

Buildings have a strong visual impact in a bare and flat landscape with a low horizon, as here at Kyle of Durness in North-West Sutherland *(Photo: Lorne Gill)*

A strong pattern of lines created by the watercourse, boundary walls, roads and tracks at Crosscleuch farm at Loch of the Lowes in Selkirkshire *(© Scottish Tourist Board)*

OPPOSITE
The crofting township of Geary on Skye, strung out along a line following the contours *(Photo: Patricia and Angus Macdonald)*

Modification of
micro-climate in a sheltered
garden at Plockton in
Wester Ross

OPPOSITE
Location of individual croft
houses at Geary in relation
to the road, field pattern and
sites of earlier settlement
*(Photo: Patricia and Angus
Macdonald)*

Lowland setting of large
scale, where the landscape
and buildings are in
proportion with each other
and siting on low ground
has avoided undue visual
intrusion

CHAPTER TWO

LOCATION
Deciding Where To Build

The location of settlements, individual farms and houses, indeed the very presence of buildings, contributes to the character of a landscape. They add diversity, act as focal points, emphasise changes in gradient, affect qualities of remoteness and become reference points from which the scale of the landscape can be assessed. This chapter deals with the many factors to be considered when choosing a site for development. Among these are the existing settlement patterns, the size and shape of the building, its relationship with the wider countryside and the uses to which the surrounding land will be put. The requirements of the development and the capacity of the landscape to absorb these are the two fundamental considerations in the choice of location. To be confident of a satisfactory solution it is essential that both are assessed together.

THE DESIGN BRIEF

Goethe once said that there are three things to be looked for in a building: that it stands on the right spot, that it be securely founded, and that it be attractively executed – and to be confident of meeting these criteria, the developer's requirements should be fully defined in a design brief.

There are generally two siting options available in the countryside. One is to find vacant land in a town or village. This has the advantage of the development becoming part of an existing community, with the cost of connection to public utility services being relatively low, and shopping and other facilities likely to be available nearby. The other option is to develop an isolated site that offers solitude and tranquillity, but here bringing in services is likely to be more expensive. In both options the potential impact of the proposed building must be considered fully from the outset, and it should be borne in mind that some highly valued landscapes may not be capable of accepting any development at all without permanent damage.

The desire for a dream project in the countryside is a common motivation for rural development. However, many such dreams have come to nought by having a building designed first, and then finding that it is ill-suited for the site. Not only does this create an eyesore detracting from the wider landscape, but it is also a lost opportunity – a lost chance to allow the design concept to be inspired by the site. This can be avoided by undertaking an analysis of the site, its landscape and of the existing pattern of built development in that landscape before plans proceed too far.

Different types of development have requirements which will influence where they may be most conveniently located, but harmony is usually best achieved in association with an existing settlement. However, it is important that the character of this settlement and its surroundings are analysed to highlight the key characteristics which give it its identity. The scale and character of a new development can then be designed to complement adjacent buildings in terms of siting and orientation and in the use of form and materials. A development should also acknowledge the gradual rate of change associated with village life. The site should be large enough to allow the building, or group of buildings, to relate to the existing spatial arrangement, and spaces which contribute to the aesthetic quality of a settlement should be left untouched, in particular village greens and other areas which enhance environmental quality. Particular care needs to be taken with sites on the edges of a settlement, as these act as a transition between built and natural surroundings.

All these considerations can be drawn together in the design brief, which should embrace key aspects discussed in this and subsequent chapters of the book. The brief should ensure that all those concerned know exactly what is expected of them, including, where applicable, the architect, landscape designer, building contractor and the various specialist trades. It

Outside settlements, the first option should be to look for redundant buildings that can be converted. Here a cottage and outbuilding have been combined into a modern dwelling near Pluscarden in Morayshire, designed by the Law & Dunbar- Nasmith Partnership *(Photo: John Foster)*

will also be helpful in discussions with the local planning authority and other public bodies with an interest in the project, as well as building societies or banks providing financial backing.

The brief should be a summary statement and needs to be flexible. It is the starting point for negotiation and should allow for change as the project progresses. The opportunities and constraints should be clearly stated, particularly any limitations on the funds available. True costs can only be determined by estimating expenditure for the whole life of the development, including both capital works and future maintenance. A distinction should be made between firm requirements and indicative suggestions so as to stimulate an inspired use of the site and to encourage high standards of design. Teamwork will also be essential to achieve an integrated approach from those involved. Although details will vary according to the type of project in hand, the basic brief should include the following:

- details of the site and location for landscape analysis and for the checking of planning policies, public utilities, and ground conditions;
- access to and egress from the site, and the pattern of circulation, including any separation between vehicles and pedestrians;
- features on the site to be protected and incorporated into the layout, such as existing trees and water features;
- views from the site and from the surrounding countryside which may influence the bulk and height of buildings;
- a schedule of accommodation and functional needs, as well as the form of construction, materials and colours to be used;
- details of external spaces, their purpose and relationship to each other and to internal spaces, and between private and public spaces;
- effects desired for outdoor surfaces and planting;
- the budget for capital works and maintenance costs for the full life of the development.

The design process can start when the information for the brief has been assembled and analysed.

An issue often facing the aspiring developer in the countryside is whether to opt for an entirely new building or to search for an old one, whether habitable or derelict, and adapt it according to requirements. The latter may not, as is commonly believed, be more expensive than an entirely new development and offers the possible bonus of maturity of setting and character of materials. However, great care must be taken to ensure that new additions are in sympathy with the architectural style of the existing structure, and a detailed design brief of the client's requirements is just as important for conversion and rehabilitation work as it is for new development.

ANALYSING LANDSCAPES

The character of an area will be a deciding factor in the best approach to any new development, and an analysis should be undertaken to find out how the different elements in the landscape relate to each other and thereby create its sense of place. Although a site may already have been chosen, analysis will pay dividends by providing a better understanding of its context within the wider landscape and will guide the design of buildings and site layout so that the development sits comfortably in, or even enhances the surroundings. Key landscape elements can be identified and used to influence the orientation, scale and shape of proposed buildings, and this will also reveal views to be enjoyed from the site, as well as views into the site from the surrounding countryside that will be important for the general amenity of the area.

There are recognised techniques of landscape analysis, including those developed and used by organisations like the Countryside Commission for Scotland, the Forestry Commission and the Forestry Service of the US Department of Agriculture. These techniques distinguish between 'spatial elements' – those elements with volume and area such as landform, water

Horizon lines, as revealed in this view of Strathfarar, are to be avoided since development straddling across or breaking such lines will appear in silhouette and is likely to have an adverse visual impact on landscape quality *(Photo: Lorne Gill)*

bodies, vegetation cover, field patterns and settlements – and 'linear elements', which include horizon and ridge lines, water courses, shelterbelts and hedgerows with trees, hedges, boundary walls and fences, and roads, railways and tracks. These elements together, by their alignment in relation to each other, make up the pattern of a landscape, but there is also a third category of 'objects', such as individual buildings, monuments, bridges, pylons, sheep stells, specimen trees and the like which are important features and focal points in determining scale as well. Similarly, other factors which govern aesthetic perception include scale and shape, diversity or uniformity, openness or enclosure, texture and colour, and the juxtaposition and interlocking of elements. It is the combination of all these aspects which makes up landscape character.

Another aspect of visual assessment is 'proximity' – the further away an observer is, the less is the apparent size of an object, the less is the relative impact, and the more likely it is that other elements in the intervening ground will be of equal importance to the view. Likewise, 'screening', the extent to which a view is obscured by intermediate objects or topography, and 'silhouette', how a feature is seen against a backdrop of landform or against the skyline, are also key considerations – as are seasonal change and

The silhouette of Dallas Dhu Distillery near Forres in Morayshire, its visual impact reduced by splitting it into smaller units *(Photo: Paul Tomkins, © Scottish Tourist Board)*

whether the direction of the view is with the light or against it, since both will affect colour and contrast.

An assessment of the landscape impact of a new development should also be undertaken from static and mobile viewpoints. 'Static' is when the site is viewed from a fixed position, which is of limited analytical value. 'Mobile' is when the site is assessed from a series of sequential points at different distances, levels and angles of approach. In sensitive areas, the visual assessment can be extended to map all points from which the development can be seen, to show the area of visibility or 'zone of visual influence'. Both static and mobile assessments can be simulated with computer-aided techniques, or by using photo-montages.

The dominant linear elements in a typical Lowland landscape are generally hedgerows, boundary walls and roads. Arable fields and pastures, interspersed with woodlands and settlements, give the landscape volume. Typically, old farm buildings are conveniently located for working the fields but set well back from the best arable land in the traditional manner. Buildings are as a rule associated with landscape elements such as shelter planting, or are located at the edge of woodlands. As long as the natural environment is allowed to dominate, buildings will appear in harmony with their setting, especially if ridges and elevated positions are avoided.

The topography of the north and west varies so much that there is no single category that can be said to typify all Highland landscapes – if there were to be one, it would be the crofting landscape. Its landform is a mixture of hills, glens and lochs, the most striking characteristic being the relative lack of trees. The uniformity of appearance is derived from bareness caused by centuries of degradation by overgrazing and a severe climate. The subtle pattern of rough and uncultivated heathland and moor, previously cultivated and abandoned areas, and the crofting land still in use leads to differences in colour and texture. The strongest feature is the settlement pattern of crofting townships, a string of houses laid out in a loose line parallel to the contours. The buildings are spread out, one or two to each croft, and the cultivated strips run in strong parallel lines from the upper communal hill grazing down to the floor of the glen or towards the shore.

The favourite locations for human settlement in Highland glens were on river terraces or at the break between the valley floor and the sloping sides. In a treeless landscape, as on the coast, it is the relationship of the landform, watercourses, boundary walls, roads and tracks which makes up the landscape character. To avoid a new building 'floating' in such a setting, it should be visually tied into one or more of these elements.

Before the introduction of piped supplies proximity to water was important, and the location of human settlements was traditionally associated with watercourses. Farms, for example, were often situated on a 'spring line' where water was readily available – this is why farms are often positioned at a similar height along a hillside. However, developments close to the edge of lochs and rivers should be avoided as buildings located on the edge of water bodies are likely to appear prominent and can easily detract from the landscape quality of an area.

SCALE AND SIZE

The scale relationship between buildings and their landscape setting is a key consideration. The size of many traditional buildings looks right because they seem to fit easily into a particular expanse of landscape – the respective sizes of buildings and landscape are said to be 'in proportion' or 'in scale' with each other. Thus, scale is a concept of relative size. Whereas size itself is absolute and can be expressed in terms of a measurement, scale is an expression of the size relationship, both horizontal and vertical, between

A bare landscape without tree cover at Elphin in North-West Sutherland against the backdrop of Suilven *(Photo: Lorne Gill)*

one object and another, and between an object and its setting. The position of the viewer relative to the observed surroundings is also a consideration, the distance and height of the viewpoint being the main variables.

The study of scale should be an integral part of the landscape analysis, and a distinction is often made between 'large-scale' and 'small-scale' landscapes. This is a reference to our perception of size relative to ourselves as viewers, and the perceived scene will also vary according to the distance and height of the viewpoint. The topography of a large-scale landscape is comprised of sweeping lines and simple shapes, and the pattern of vegetation is often uniform with few objects to break the landform. A common feature of large-scale landscapes in Scotland is the presence of extensive areas of water in sea and inland lochs. However, the topography of a small-scale landscape is made up of a mixture of smaller, more irregular features, such as valleys, hills and undulations. The vegetation is varied, and the presence of objects and field boundaries breaks down the outline of the landform. When, for example, the viewpoint is at a low level so that visibility is restricted to the near distance, the observed surroundings are characterised by topography and vegetation that create a sense of enclosure. If objects such as trees, hedgerows, boundary walls and buildings break up the scale to provide a multiplicity of reference points for the viewer, a landscape can then be said to be small-scale.

Buildings can reinforce, exaggerate or destroy existing scale. As a general rule, large buildings are likely to be compatible with large-scale landscapes, while small buildings are appropriate in small-scale landscapes. However, scale can be adjusted by manipulating bulk or shape, by rearranging elements such as windows and doors, and by the choice of

Scourie in Sutherland, a settlement located on low-lying ground to take advantage of the natural shelter in the lee of the surrounding hills *(Photo: Lorne Gill)*

materials and use of colour.

Skill is required to create the right size or scale relationship between a building and its landscape setting when the natural scales of each are at variance. Wherever possible, it is best to choose a site where suitable reference points already exist, then relate buildings to the scale of these features. In large-scale landscapes, where few features are present to serve as reference points, a new building can be very intrusive. An elongated shape located on low ground may be acceptable, but the character of a bare landscape of stark simplicity can be easily destroyed by the presence of any human artefact. When buildings of large bulk have to be located in small-scale landscapes, adjustment to built form may be necessary to minimise visual impact. This can be done by designing the buildings as a series of smaller units rather than one large single block or, it can be achieved by the application of colour to help reduce apparent bulk.

CLIMATE

Climate has been a dominant influence on the traditional siting and form of settlements. In comparison with the rest of the United Kingdom, Scotland experiences greater seasonal temperature differences, higher wind speeds with more driving rain and snow, larger variations in the length of day, and a sun lower in the sky. The west is windier and wetter, the east is drier and colder, while parts of the central Grampians experience sub-arctic conditions. For building purposes, climate should be considered for the environment of a region (macro-climate), for the environment of a locality

The contorted shapes of Scots pines hugging the ground in an exposed coastal location at Yellowcraig in East Lothian
(Photo: Ruth Grant)

Buildings were traditionally set back some distance from the water's edge, as here at Achnambeithach in Glencoe
(Photo: John W. Mackay)

or settlement (meso-climate), and for the environment of a site (micro-climate). Indeed, differences can be observed over only a few hundred metres, where altitude, direction of slope (aspect) and tree shelter combine to create noticeable variations in exposure.

An understanding of climate is necessary to design a sensible site layout. Signs to look for in field observation are the distorted shape of trees, indicating the direction and ferocity of the prevailing wind, and the stunted growth of trees and shrubs on hilltops, indicating higher wind speeds due to exposed landform. Verdant vegetation on sheltered slopes indicates good soil capability and improved growth where wind speeds are lower, and frost hollows and mist accumulation in valley bottoms reflect the tendency for calm and cold air to sink. Moss growth on stone walls indicates a high degree of masonry saturation in certain locations, and the position of sheep stells indicates locations where drifting snow will not lie.

An understanding of the effect of climate can also be obtained by studying earlier settlements. Exposed ridges and hilltops have traditionally been avoided, as have frost hollows and locations in the shadow of hills, while locations part way up a hillside on a southern slope have been favoured. Buildings were often linked to the landscape with tree planting, hedges and boundary walls, which helped to reduce wind speed and, depending on exposure, views and orientation, shelterbelt planting was also a common feature. Such manipulation of the micro-climate for human settlement helped to create an underlying harmony between buildings and landscape.

This approach will show similar benefits if applied to modern layout design. Building groups located in warm, sheltered localities will provide a more comfortable external environment for people to enter and leave, for sitting out and for easier garden cultivation. Wind noise and heat loss will be reduced, resulting in energy saving and greater comfort. Shelter may be further enhanced with tree and shrub planting, and boundary walls and fencing, leaving the more exposed parts of the site for other important functions, such as access roads, sewerage plant and storage.

PLANNING AND OTHER PROTECTION

The process of finding a suitable location should include a visit to the local planning authority, preferably at an early stage, to find out about land-use policies. At a regional level the structure plan will provide information on strategic policies for roads, industry, housing, education and environmental protection. Policies will be stated in broad land-use terms and priorities given for action and expenditure in the years ahead. Local plans, however, are more detailed and will specify the extent and nature of land-use. They provide the basis for development control, and individual planning applications are determined according to these policies. An inspection of structure and local plans will reveal where development can, or cannot, take place and what kind of restrictions might apply in any given location.

As part of the planning system, or closely associated with it, there are a number of protective procedures of which all developers should be aware. Buildings of architectural or historical value are statutorily listed by the Secretary of State, and if new development is thought likely to affect the setting of listed buildings the local planning authority should be consulted. Indeed, it may be necessary to advertise the proposals for development when these lie within the curtilage of a listed building, a requirement obviated only when the curtilage is very large and when the new development does not interfere with the views of the listed building. Even new buildings outwith the curtilage, but which would seriously restrict the views of a listed building, or rise above it so that its silhouette can no longer be seen unobscured from familiar viewpoints, should be regarded as adversely affecting the setting. If many listed buildings occur together, the whole group may be designated a Conservation Area where new development is strictly controlled. Other protective procedures include Tree Preservation Orders, which are issued to protect important woodland features, and the scheduling of archaeological sites as Ancient Monuments. Fines can be imposed if the protected objects are destroyed or their setting adversely affected in any way by a new development.

There are a number of special land-use designations which protect particular aspects of our environmental heritage and within which the scale and type of permitted development is restricted. Advice on where these designations apply can, in the first instance, be obtained from the relevant local authority. They include Green Belts, which are intended to stop the outward expansion of large towns, prevent built-up areas coalescing, and protect the rural setting of urban communities. Similarly, Regional and Country Parks are often found near to major urban settlements and have been planned to provide opportunities for recreation and conservation, while to protect areas of high scenic value many local authorities have designated Areas of Great Landscape Value. Outstanding landscapes are designated by the Secretary of State according to their national value as National Scenic Areas, National Parks or equivalents. To protect wildlife sites of special importance within an area, Local Nature Reserves are established by local authorities, while habitats of regional and national significance are designated by the Nature Conservancy Council as Sites of Special Scientific Interest and National Nature Reserves. Some of these designations will allow new development, but normally with special conditions attached to planning permissions. In others, the natural heritage value may be so important, and the environment so sensitive, that new buildings would be unacceptable.

It is important to note that the planning system and designations outlined above should be regarded as positive guidance towards good practice rather than as negative constraints. The government and business community are also now increasingly embracing the concept of sustainable development in their policies. This concept is based on the principle that resources should be used to meet the needs of people today in such a manner that the same resources will continue to fulfil the needs of future generations. The principles set out below and at the end of subsequent chapters provide guidance on how to build in ways that are sustainable in ecological, aesthetic and cultural terms. When deciding where to build, the first principle is to take an integrated approach to the environment. All facets of the countryside are interdependent and this is the only way to ensure that the natural order and built development are kept in balance.

CHAPTER THREE

SETTING
Fitting Into The Landscape

The setting of a building acts as a transition area or link between the building and the surrounding landscape, and great care is required if the integrity of the setting is not to be destroyed by locating the building or other elements of the development on inappropriate parts of the site. This calls for an integrated approach, for unless the whole development is designed with due regard to all adjoining landscape features, the character and visual quality of a locality is likely to be adversely affected. This is where so much modern development goes wrong in that there is a failure to plan and design both buildings and outdoor space together. Too often building design is seen as a separate exercise with other elements of the development as an afterthought. This chapter offers guidance on placing buildings in the most appropriate parts of a site and explains how external features such as boundary walls and fences, water features and planting can be used to enhance a setting.

WORKING WITH THE CONTOURS

Together with field observation, some familiarity with the interpretation and use of maps is necessary when analysing a site for new development. The relief of landform is denoted by contours, which are lines drawn to show height intervals that provide the means of visualising the site in three dimensions. The magnitude of intervals varies according to the scale of the map used, and gradients are usually expressed either as a ratio of horizontal run to vertical rise (e.g. 1:4), or vertical rise as a percentage of horizontal run.

The siting of a building in relation to landform, the alignment of a building relative to the direction of a slope, whether disturbance of natural landform through earthworks is required, and the elevation of a building relative to its surroundings all require thought. Although there are historical examples of prominent buildings in elevated positions that look well settled into their surroundings, their visual impact is often ameliorated by planting that has taken generations to mature. This type of elevated siting on ridges and hilltops should be avoided for new development. Most requirements, like a good view, sunlight, shelter, privacy and easy access, can be met in locations where the building is tucked into folds of the land.

A strong common feature throughout the Scottish countryside is the

OPPOSITE
Balvaird Castle, near Glenfarg, is a tall building in a prominent position, yet it sits comfortably in the landscape because it is masked by mature planting and the contours have not been disrupted so that the ground sweeps naturally up to the walls *(Photo: Lorne Gill)*

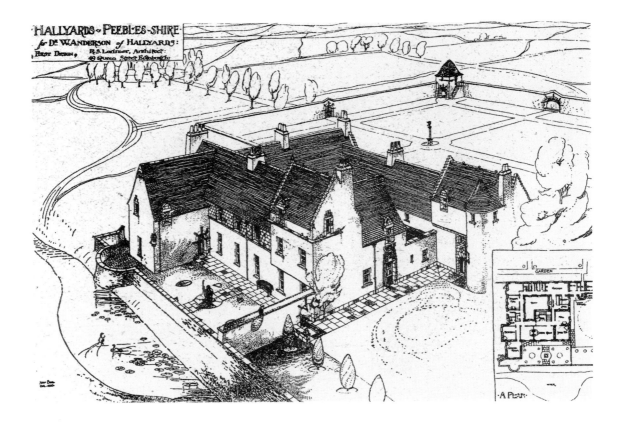

HALLYARDS · PEEBLES·SHIRE
for Dr W. ANDERSON of HALLYARDS:
First Design, R. S. Lorimer, Architect:
49 Queen Street Edinburgh

·A·PLAN·

This is how Sir Robert Lorimer intended Hallyards in Peeblesshire to look in its landscape setting. On one side the rooms look on to a small courtyard with water beyond; on the opposite side is a larger walled garden with a formal layout – thereby extending the building into the landscape in two directions by boundary walls. The other two sides have direct contact with the undulating Borders countryside, and the overall effect is of intertwining the building with its setting (© RCAHMS)

manner in which both settlements and individual buildings have been positioned in relation to landform. Buildings have generally been aligned parallel to the contours, although in certain circumstances individual units were set deliberately at a right angle to the slope to punctuate part of a development or to use the slope to provide access to a building at different levels. As settlements expanded, the upper limit of built development would generally rise on concave slopes and fall on convex ground in the same manner as the line of tree cover. There has been a traditional preference for sites on low ground and in folds of hills, but for obvious reasons frost hollows and areas subject to flooding have been avoided.

Sloping sites are the most difficult to handle because the construction methods now used can lead too easily to the creation of an unsightly, large level platform. In the past, manual methods meant that floor levels were stepped to keep earthworks to a minimum, and this produced a building profile that reflected natural ground shapes. Modern machinery has changed this and it is now normal to bulldoze a platform to accommodate the whole building on a single level. This is difficult to achieve with a satisfactory visual result since the outcome is an artificially elevated building with unnaturally graded cuttings and embankments. There are no practical reasons why the floor levels of even a standard building kit should not be stepped to fit into an existing slope, and varied floor levels will almost

BRIGLANDS · KINROSS-SHIRE
FOR J·AVON CLYDE ESQ· R·S·LORIMER ARCHT
49 QUEEN STREET·EDINR

GROUND FLOOR PLAN

Bridgelands in Kinross-shire, another example of Lorimer's integrated approach to architecture and landscape design. The key lesson here is his use of levels on a sloping site. On either side of the projecting wing the ground has been cut to create a sunken garden and a courtyard forming outdoor rooms at ground-floor level. The entrance road is also sunk to this level and artfully terminated at the gate around an ornamental tree (© RCAHMS)

certainly provide a more interesting design of both internal and external spaces. When a large level platform is absolutely essential, it is important to strike a proper balance between cut and fill, and to ensure that the site is large enough to allow new slopes to be blended naturally with the shape of the surrounding ground.

There are two options for positioning buildings on a platform. If positioned at the back, level ground in front of the building will be left that may command good views, but it is likely to be exposed unless planted with trees and hedges or walled to provide shelter. If positioned at the front of the platform, private and sheltered space can be formed between the building and the shape of the cut ground. This was the traditional solution which, combined with stepped levels, can be an effective way of creating pleasant spaces and settling built development into a landscape.

If there is surplus material it can be used to mould the ground to form a good visual relationship between the base of a building and existing ground levels, with the added benefit of avoiding costly removal. Modification of the landform may be required to reinforce the setting of the building, or to relate it more clearly to the landscape. For example, larger developments may require a complete modification of landform by lowering the buildings

into the site to reduce their visual impact. Raising the surrounding ground levels will often have the added advantage of screening artefacts at lower level, while allowing the main elements of the building to be expressed clearly. In all cases where it is necessary to modify the existing landform, gradients and shapes should be inspired by the surrounding landscape and the surface must be restored to blend with it. It is therefore essential to ensure that sufficient land is available for this purpose. Analysis of soil type and the selection of seed mixtures and plant species that are compatible with local ground cover are also important considerations.

The position of vehicular and pedestrian access into a site will be subject to control by the local highway authority, but within the site itself the route alignment should be selected to fit into the landscape as well as satisfying functional needs. The most economical solution may appear to be the shortest distance between the site boundary and the building. However, this could involve large amounts of expensive cut and fill and can be unsightly on sloping ground. Ideally, road and path alignments should be related to landform, although gradient and alignment can, with care, be varied to create interest and enhance the approach to a building.

SITE BOUNDARIES

Another strong feature of traditional buildings was the method of boundary treatment. The same local stone was normally used for both buildings and boundaries. Within a settlement, walls tied the buildings together into tight clusters and often enclosed gardens and inbye fields so that a settlement became interwoven with the pattern of the wider landscape. Link-walls between a house and its outbuildings helped to unify them into a cohesive group and create a pleasant composition (see pp 102–3). Stone was also commonly used for retaining walls on sloping ground to create flat terraces and to achieve a good relationship between outdoor and indoor space. This treatment is an attractive feature of many coastal villages.

Stone walling is an ancient craft that is becoming popular once more, and it need not be more costly than using modern materials. It can give local character to a development and, when carefully aligned in relation to the contours, it can provide shelter and screening in circumstances where trees are inappropriate or will take too long to become effective. It is also useful in linking new buildings to an existing development. However, it is very important to respect the shape of the land and thereby avoid boundaries which do not relate to the pattern of the surrounding landscape. As with the architectural form and detailing of the buildings themselves, careful observation of existing walls and their construction techniques will provide clues for what is appropriate for the site in question.

Unsightly platform created by cut-and-fill for a building set at right angles to the contours (top). Same building aligned parallel to the contours with a terraced platform, which reduces visual impact (middle). Same amount of accommodation split into three separate units to lessen apparent bulk and to reduce the need for cut-and-fill (bottom) *(Drawings: Reinhard Behrens)*

Intrusive appearance of kit-house with unduly high underbuilding (top). How the visual impact can be reduced by a lean-to garage and the stair being turned round to follow the slope of the ground (bottom)
(Drawings: Reinhard Behrens)

In some cases, fences may be appropriate, for example in an open landscape where there is no local tradition of stone walling or hedging. In these circumstances it is again important to choose techniques and materials which are in keeping with the character of the area. Often a simple post-and-wire fence will be all that is needed, with the addition of netting where stock-proofing is necessary. The use of high-tensile spring steel wire greatly reduces the number of posts and hence the landscape impact of the fence: 'ranch-type' fences with horizontal boarding are rarely appropriate in the countryside. A traditional form of boundary, now rarely used, is the 'ha-ha', and this solution is worth considering where it is desirable to maintain a clear view to and from a building.

WATER FEATURES

There is a long tradition of creating ornamental lakes and ponds as part of designed landscapes around country houses. Many such houses had curling ponds, reservoirs and fish ponds which, as well as being pleasing to the eye, often also provided a source of food. Many farms had reservoirs for water power before the introduction of electricity, but water features also provide important wildlife habitats and there has been a recent trend in creating ponds for this purpose.

If, in formulating the design brief, the creation of a new pond is thought desirable, the purpose should be made clear. It may have a single purpose, such as for a wildlife habitat, or for boating or fishing by damming a watercourse, or simply for a water garden or amenity to enhance the setting of the built development, but it may be possible to combine several of these, and the siting, layout, water depth and choice of aquatic plants should be specified accordingly. Its value to wildlife and aesthetic appeal will be enhanced if the water body is connected to other landscape features such as shelterbelts, hedges, stone walls and ditches. For most applications, the placing of water features on a site must be carried out with careful regard to levels and contours so that the result appears natural. If earthworks are required to remodel the ground, new contours should blend naturally with the surrounding landform.

If a site contains, or is next to, water, its source, quality, outfall and flood levels need to be surveyed as the construction of nearby buildings can have a significant effect on the existing pattern of land drainage and ground-water levels. All these considerations require a detailed knowledge of the contours for the whole water catchment area, including any implications that the alterations to waterflow might have for owners downstream of a proposed development. Another consideration in the design and layout of water features is safety, as children are always attracted to water. For this reason, and to minimise visual impact, buildings should be set back from the water's edge – unless special design consider-ations demand otherwise and special care is taken. Small streams and burns, if used creatively, can do much to enhance the setting of buildings and should be diverted or concealed in culverts only as a last resort.

PLANTING

Planting around built development can have several purposes, but the main reason in Scotland is to create enclosure for shelter. In his advice to the Scottish gardener in 1683, John Reid was quite emphatic on this point, saying 'there is no Countrey can have more need of planting than this, so non more needfull of Inclosing: for we well know how vain it is to plant unless we Inclose.' His prescription for how to perform this task was: 'if the ground be level, plant such Trees as grow lowest, at the South-side, and still higher by degrees towards the North, that the talest and strongest may be on the North-side; so shall the Northern blasts be guarded off, and the Sunbeames the better received in amongst them.'

Planting can also be used as a barrier – for privacy, to screen and delineate spaces in a site layout, to keep out noise and to provide safety for work activities, sport, games or children's play – and as with water, it can also help to introduce diversity for both visual pleasure and wildlife habitat. New planting should be designed to link a development with existing features in the landscape, and thereby help to integrate buildings with their surroundings. To succeed in this, native species are recommended, although there are circumstances where it may be appropriate to use exotic species for ornamental trees.

Existing trees should be regarded as an important asset and surveys will establish their age and health so that an assessment can be made of their potential use within a new site layout. The position, scale, shape and species of new planting should echo those of surrounding woodland cover. Care is required when planting close to buildings where the ultimate height of the species used must be known, and this requires a knowledge of soil and local climate. New trees alongside a building look small when young, but they may grow into dominant features in time (see pp 108–9). In this way, scale can be manipulated by planting large trees near to small buildings to enhance the scale of their setting or vice versa, but, in all circumstances, it is important that a site is planned at the outset with sufficient space for trees to grow to maturity. When trees are planted close to buildings, care must be taken to ensure that their roots do not damage foundations or services, and it must also be borne in mind that mature tree canopies will cast shadows.

Trees are too often thought of as a means of concealing problems that have been caused by misguided positioning of buildings or by poor architectural design, and attempting to ameliorate such failings can easily

Visual impact can be
reduced by lowering a large
development into a site –
Lagavulin Distillery on Islay
*(Photo: Paul Tomkins, Scottish
Tourist Board)*

make matters worse if inappropriate solutions are used. For example, a row
of trees around the perimeter of a site may expose any design inadequacies
by drawing attention to them. On the other hand, well-placed planting
outside the site to screen important views may well be more effective, while
by far the best way to soften the outline of a development is judicious
planting within the site itself, allowing certain parts to be framed or
highlighted and others to be screened, adding additional texture and colour
contrast. Similarly, well-positioned planting can often help simplify a
complicated arrangement of building elements into a more pleasing
composition and also help break up the scale of a large development.

Tree planting on the windward side of a site will give overall shelter,

The horizontal
configuration of boundary
walls and animal enclosures
is as much a part of the
architecture as the buildings
themselves on this farm near
Glenelg *(Photo: Lorne Gill)*

The ornamental pond enhances the setting of the museum building at Kelburn Country Centre in Ayrshire. Clad in corrugated iron, the museum was built in 1898 by the 7th Earl of Glasgow to house his New Zealand collection after returning from serving as Governor there (© *Earl of Glasgow*)

The size of an oak tree when planted, after ten years and when reaching 100 years (*Drawing: Reinhard Behrens*)

making the building warmer and more energy efficient as well as outdoor spaces more pleasant – a shelterbelt can reduce wind speeds by 15–30 per cent, depending on its area, density and height. A mixed woodland of deciduous and coniferous trees gives the best effect and will reduce wind speeds over a wide area, whilst a dense belt of evergreens will produce a small area of calm immediately on its leeward side, but bring a wider zone of air turbulence. Where shadow is a problem, deciduous windbreaks will allow more light in winter when the sun is low and the leaves have fallen.

However, the selection of species for windbreaks or shelter planting, as well as the shape of planted areas, must be designed so that they are effective, while also reflecting the character of the surrounding landscape. A mixture of broadleaf and conifer trees will, in most cases, create a comfortable visual and climatic transition between the wider landscape and built development. In exposed areas conifers can be used as a nurse crop to provide early shelter where the long-term aim is a broadleaf character.

On a large site, trees can be used to create the basic structure and framework for other categories of planting and ground cover:

- shrubs can be used as an understorey in woodlands, as hedges (cut or uncut) for barriers and edging for fruit and flowers, and to delineate spaces;
- grass, cut or left rough, is the most common treatment to provide unity in the surroundings of built development;
- herbaceous perennials and annual bedding plants can be used to decorate spaces and provide colour and textual variety.

When designing outdoor spaces it is important to adopt a positive approach, with a clear idea of the character and atmosphere to be created. The layout could be informal to create a natural extension of the surrounding countryside with the same types of ground cover extending right up to the building. Alternatively, a more formal layout could be adopted, with strong geometric divisions marking out ornamental areas, lawns, circulation space and parking, but it is then important to avoid introducing an urban effect or incurring much higher maintenance costs.

The natural environment is dynamic and subject to ever-changing and interconnected processes, and the layout and maintenance procedures for site planting have to be designed accordingly. The lifespan of plants varies, as does the speed of establishment for different types, and the consequent needs for upkeep are key considerations. For example, lawns and areas of bedding plants are quick to become established for instant effect but they require constant maintenance, whilst trees and shrubs take longer to grow but need less attention. Thus, the maintenance plan is as important as the planting plan itself, and it is essential that the design brief deals fully with this aspect of the project.

Cut hedges, like this topiary at Crathes in Aberdeenshire, show what can be done with planting to create barriers for enclosure, to define circulation patterns and to extend an architectural effect to outdoor spaces
(Photo: John Foster)

The use of trees to provide focal points or define outdoor spaces, combined with different surface treatments of grass, herbaceous plants and shrubs in the form of cut box hedges, as seen here at Drummond Castle

FITTING INTO THE LANDSCAPE

1. The whole site should be considered as an entity, with all elements of the development – buildings and outdoor spaces – being planned together.

2. Buildings generally blend best with the landscape if aligned parallel to the contours.

3. Platforms on sloping sites should be kept to a minimum, and new levels designed to fit into the surrounding landform.

4. Outdoor space should be designed so that the countryside appears to flow into the site.

5. Stone walls used for shelter and enclosure will give local character and help to tie buildings into the landscape.

6. The layout and design of new buildings should respect local tradition and settlement pattern.

7. Water and ornamental ponds can enhance settings and add wildlife interest.

8. Plants and seed mixtures should be compatible with local ground cover.

9. Design of planting should reflect the local woodland pattern, and existing trees should be retained with new planting for their succession.

10. A planting plan should be agreed, specifying establishment time, ultimate size of trees and the management regimes for different types of ground cover.

The main gate to Fort George near Inverness, built by the Adam Brothers (1748–69), whose family name is associated with the finest architecture Scotland has ever produced. Recent restoration work at the fort has been carried out under the supervision of the Law & Dunbar-Nasmith Partnership

Designed to accommodate one person, the telephone kiosk represents actual human scale. Here its roofline coincides with the lintel of the ground-floor windows *(Photo: Lorne Gill)*

CHAPTER FOUR
FORM AND LAYOUT

This chapter moves the reader from the wider countryside setting and site planning to consider the architectural treatment of buildings and the detailed design of spaces around them. The emphasis is on how buildings and external spaces can be integrated to achieve a sense of place that is appropriate for the countryside.

Much helpful information relevant to this chapter can be found in *The Rural Architecture of Scotland* by Alexander Fenton and Bruce Walker, and in *Buildings of the Scottish Countryside* by Robert J. Naismith, as well as in the many rural architectural guide books published by the Royal Incorporation of Architects in Scotland. Readers are also recommended to consult the work of the North American writer Christopher Alexander, whose several books are germaine to what follows.

LANDSCAPE DESIGN

The traditional approach to landscape design in Scotland has been governed by an understanding of nature and working in harmony with the land. A respect for climate, together with a need for shelter and enclosure, have been the key criteria. For the renaissance architect, the house was the focal point, and John Reid's advice was to 'Situate your House in a healthy Soyl, near to a fresh-spring, defended from the Impetuous west winds, northern colds and eastern blasts: and mind regularity, viz Make all the Buildings and Plantings ly so about the House, as that the House may be the centre; all the Walks, Trees and Hedges running to the House'. In later romantic and picturesque designs, however, the scenic qualities of the landscape beyond the formal garden were exploited by focusing on distant views of hills, crags or architectural features.

The appearance of designed landscapes changed dramatically in the second half of the 19th century with the introduction of exotic species of plants brought back from overseas by Scottish collectors. It is hard to believe that the Rhododendrons and Azaleas, now such a familiar sight in many parts of the country, are recent importations. They were used to enhance woodland walks or emphasise striking natural landscape features, and for many people have come to typify the designed Scottish landscape. Indeed, such plants have thrived in damp and acid conditions and have greatly widened the range of plant material available, although some, like *Rhododendron ponticum*, can be

Traditional layout and use of plants in a cottage garden on Brora *(Photo: Eric Thorburn, © Highlands & Islands Enterprise)*

intrusive and have become a pest in certain areas.

Gardens and designed landscapes from different periods, particularly those attached to historic houses, have had a strong influence on later designs, but the cost of creating and maintaining such landscapes is now beyond the means of most owners. Nowadays the main opportunities for large-scale work tend to be associated with the building of new company headquarters, office and business parks and new rural settlements. With few exceptions it has unfortunately become difficult in recent years to discern an approach worthy of our Georgian and Victorian heritage. This is often due to large sites being developed piecemeal, without an adequate master plan to express the overall landscape strategy, and urban or suburban solutions being mistakenly transported to the countryside.

For small-scale designs, useful lessons can be learned from the traditional garden treatment of ordinary country houses and cottages, which often had a small enclosed ornamental garden at the front and vegetable plot and drying-green at the rear. Sometimes only a narrow roadside strip was available and walls were used for climbing plants, but the visual effect was striking and attractive (see p 147). Boundary walls and surface materials were used to give a clear definition of space for different functions, and the layout used strong geometrical shapes, with symmetry in appropriate places, making it easy to see points of access to both spaces and buildings. Surface and plant materials were chosen to minimise maintenance: longevity was required for plants providing the framework of the garden, while shrubs and herbaceous plants gave seasonal colour.

A key lesson from traditional practice is the need for unity between building and landscape design, and for spaces within buildings to be related to the use of outdoor spaces to secure functional and visual integration. Some key principles from traditional Scottish practice are that:

- lines of movement and points of access can be emphasised by using symmetry: although the arrangements of these elements in an asymmetrical or informal layout can be equally successful, it is less easy to achieve;
- each area should have surface materials appropriate for its use, but there should not be unnecessary subdivision as this will cause both perceived and actual loss of usable space;
- climbing plants on external walls can enhance the visual appearance and integration, and this technique can also serve to modify the micro-climate;
- the clarity of visual effect is fundamental, and the range of plant and hard surface materials should be kept to a minimum in the overall design to avoid visual clutter and to ensure that maintenance regimes are simple and straightforward.

There is no distinct style of landscape design today that can serve as a single guide for new developments in the countryside. The formal and picturesque styles of the past are still relevant, but during this century there has been a strong Japanese influence, and the Modern Movement in architecture has encouraged the use of free form. The abstraction in modern paintings has also left its mark. Against this background there are some specific modern trends, such as to use plants to express shape, colour and texture in an informal manner, rather than regimenting them into strict patterns. Native species are often used in preference to exotic ones, and herb-rich seed mixtures have become popular as an alternative to traditional lawn grasses. Natural objects like large rocks and boulders are sometimes used for ornamental purposes in place of traditional statuary, although some designers have in recent years revived the formal styles of the past.

The work of the landscape architect Sylvia Crowe has done much to influence modern design philosophy, and in *Garden Design* she stresses the need to create a strong sense of unity by:

- a clear theme of design to reflect intended purpose and use of spaces;
- the congruity of landform so that ground shapes flow freely through the site;
- restricting the range of surface materials to give cohesion, and permitting one type of vegetation to dominate;
- arranging divisions to balance closed and open spaces, and to govern light and shade;
- using the colour and texture in plants and surfaces to create visual effects.

Crowe distinguishes between 'introverted' and 'extroverted' gardens. An introverted garden occurs when the design sets out to create inward-looking spaces that will provide visual interest within the site boundaries, and she explains that 'in a small garden a fine tree or piece of sculpture may be enough to form the focal point to which all else is subordinate'. A common approach is to borrow several thematic features from illustrations in plant catalogues or gardening books, or even from historic gardens, and squeeze these into the confined space of a small domestic garden. But each thematic feature depends on a certain amount of space for its effect, and a small garden is rarely capable of accommodating more than one without a loss of unity, or creating a suburban character and a confusing visual effect. An extroverted garden, on the other hand, occurs when the design provides outward-looking views of the surrounding countryside. The design brief should specify which approach is preferred or is relevant to local site conditions.

LAYOUT OF SPACES

A formal design style may be most appropriate next to buildings, and can be used to articulate spaces and emphasise the qualities of the site. These can be arranged to form suntraps, provide privacy, create safe areas for children's play and so on. The relationship between the internal and external use of space should be an integral part of the design process, allowing easy access from the appropriate rooms of the house to external spaces such as vegetable gardens, outdoor eating areas, driveways and patios. Layout and design should mirror this interaction of functions so that hard surfaces and geometric lines may predominate in the areas around the house, with a more informal design style as the garden area extends into the surrounding countryside.

Layout planning should start with a consideration of people's perceptions and in *Site Planning*, Kevin Lynch has identified some helpful guiding principles:

- a person can be recognised at 30 metres and a space becomes impersonal when larger than this, while a person's features and expressions can be recognised at 15 metres, this being the maximum for an 'intimate' space;
- when the largest dimension of a building equals the distance from the eye, it is difficult to see the whole structure; when it is twice the distance from the eye the whole building can be seen; when it is three times the distance from the eye, a building can be seen in relation to others in, say, a terrace; and when it is more than four times the distance away a building becomes part of the general scene;
- the most comfortable space is when wall height is between a third and a half of the horizontal width; and there is little sense of enclosure when the height is less than a quarter of the width.

Development within or on the edge of a settlement should follow the pattern of layout that is characteristic of the area, and this varies a great deal for different parts of the country. For example, the layout of crofting townships in the north and west of Scotland is simple but with a well-defined relationship to landform. Sometimes the buildings are loosely strung out in a varied topography, whilst elsewhere they follow a single line along the sweeping contours of a large-scale landscape. The absence of tree cover and other artefacts makes it very important that the position and layout of new buildings fits into this pattern. It is also essential to follow the traditional pattern for spaces around these buildings. Apart from walled enclosures for animals and gardens, the arrangement is simple: the surrounding ground normally sweeps uninterrupted up to walls and

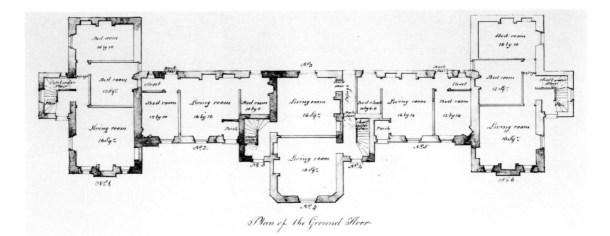

Plan of the Ground Floor

buildings and the whole countryside is the outdoor space.

Using the existing layout for clues is equally important in a Lowland setting, but here the pattern is very different. Settlements have a stronger urban character with a street pattern that governs overall layout. Unity of street appearance is achieved by conforming to a traditional building line. The bulk of the building, as part of a row or terrace, has traditionally provided the barrier between public and private space (see p 116, top). If it is set back from the pavement, there may be sufficient room for private space at the front that requires screening from the street by hedging, walling or fencing. However, if adjoining properties have front gardens, it is incompatible to use this space for parking. Private space at the back, on the other hand, can be planned according to the requirements of the development, making sure that there is a proper separation of pedestrian and vehicular circulation, with any subdivision of spaces by roads and paths being kept to a minimum.

A widely acknowledged principle of layout planning is to ensure that every part of the site has a clear purpose, in both functional and visual terms. A mistake frequently made is to place a building in the middle of a site – effectively dividing it into several small parts – or on the most attractive part. However, a position near the edge would enable the whole site to be treated both functionally and visually as one large space, so

Elevation and plan of six terraced cottages designed by the architect Robert Dickson of Edinburgh in 1840 for Blair Atholl village (© *His Grace the Duke of Atholl*)

The windows are the eyes of a building – like the human face, its beauty will be affected by loss of original bits of the anatomy *(Photo: Lorne Gill)*

whenever possible a position should be chosen that allows the best part of a site to be used as an outdoor space and, when appropriate, to form a natural extension to public rooms.

Unfortunately, the layout pattern of much recent housing has tended to follow a dispersed model, derived from principles advocated by Ebenezer Howard in his influential book of 1902, *Garden Cities of Tomorrow*. The original idea was to provide a living environment with green open space to contrast with the harsh urban environment created during the Industrial Revolution. The streets were to be wide and flanked by avenues of trees, and each dwelling was to be set in an ample, leafy garden. The only venture to emulate this idea in Scotland was by A. H. Mottram in 1919, when he designed the 'Rosyth Garden Village' in Fife. Apart from some subsequent local authority housing of good quality, much residential development by the private sector has departed from this model into an unstructured suburban sprawl that now pervades both the form and layout of new housing developments throughout Britain. As Richard England has pointed out, 'architecture which started as a path to enlightenment, has ended up as a route to speculation'.

It has produced extensive low-density housing-schemes lacking in architectural quality and characterised by a meandering system of roads with dwellings set in the middle of each plot without boundary enclosure. There is much open grass but few trees so the general impression is bleak, with a lack of distinction between private and public space. This approach is demanding in its consumption of land, the indiscriminate spread of residential development is visually intrusive, and the absence of enclosure results in an uncongenial living environment.

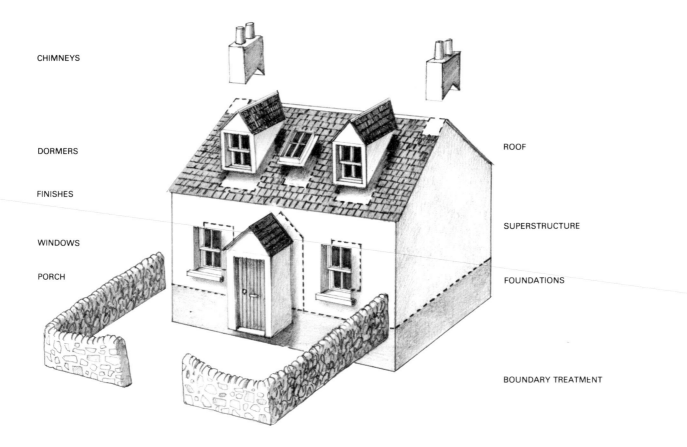

CHIMNEYS

DORMERS

FINISHES

WINDOWS

PORCH

ROOF

SUPERSTRUCTURE

FOUNDATIONS

BOUNDARY TREATMENT

A better basis for planning groups of new buildings is upon the range of different types of layout that have evolved locally to prove their suitability in a northern climate. The traditional farm steading is a good model with several plan permutations, the simplest of which is the single terrace. This represents the basic building block which can be arranged in partially enclosed spaces on an L- or U-shaped plan, or into a fully enclosed courtyard.

BUILT FORM

Traditional buildings vary greatly in their detail from region to region, but the response to climate and the use of a limited range of materials has established a robust vernacular tradition which is easily recognisable as Scottish. The early 'white' houses of the Western Isles, which evolved from the black house, serve as a good reference point from which to trace its evolution (see p 38, bottom). These included formal elements like symmetry, and a regular, geometrical pattern, as in the centrally positioned door and flanking windows.

The whole is greater than the sum of its parts, appearance being determined by how individual components are put together into an overall composition. The main elements of built form are the roof, the superstructure which encloses internal spaces, the shape and proportions of openings for doors and windows, porches and extensions, the position and shape of chimneys and the texture and colour of external finishes. The relationship to the site is determined by the foundations and underbuilding on a sloping site, and by the style and materials used in the treatment of boundaries *(Drawing: Reinhard Behrens)*

The typical rural house evolved from this during the 19th century. It was rectangular and narrow, often with only one room from front to back. It had a pitched roof with gables and a central ridge, the slope rarely falling below 35 degrees whether it was covered by slate, stone or tiles. A relatively low ground-to-eaves height, with a notable absence of under-building, gave such houses a horizontal emphasis, tying them well into the landscape. Although two-storey houses were common, the archetypal form was of one and a half storeys, with upper-level accommodation under a roof that had dormer windows. Compared to modern equivalents, this is still the most cost-effective and space-efficient architectural form in relation to volume, wall and roof surfaces, foundations and energy use. The simple, strong profile, and the impression of solidity, epitomises the rural Scottish dwelling. Even in examples where thatch or slate has given way to corrugated metal or felt, the visual effect can still be pleasing. This suggests that if proportions and the overall shape of the building are correct, there is scope for different construction techniques with a variety of materials, provided the scale is also correct and the materials are used in a functional and consistent manner.

Scale is a fundamental element of built form, and the scale of these early vernacular house-types springs from their function as human shelter and the essential economy that was applied in their construction to perform this function. Scale, as defined in Chapter 2, is the relationship between one object and another, which is here applied to the relative size of a building and the human form. In *Scottish Townscapes*, Colin McWilliam cites the sentry-box and the telephone kiosk as examples of enclosed space designed to accommodate a single individual. This observation is helpful as an illustration of human scale, since the top of a kiosk located next to single-storey cottages is level with the eaves and about the same size as the door openings. It is, in fact, so close to the scale of the buildings that it is only the contrasting colour that makes it noticeable as a separate object.

Across the range of different types and different sizes of buildings, the architect will deploy certain stylistic techniques for handling scale. With reference to Georgian terraces, McWilliam observes that:

> . . . columns and piers and pilasters provided a system, sometimes structural and sometimes ornamental, that brought together all sorts of sizes of buildings and their parts under common rules of proportion, so that in a sense these elements are stand-ins for people; the only comparable system, as we have seen, is based on the human figure. The columns of a doorpiece are of human scale, but if these same elements are applied two storeys tall to a terrace of private houses they will give it a larger, corporate scale.

According to McWilliam, human scale implies domestic scale, since most people acquire their idea of scale from the places where they live, as well as from the natural environment. Corporate scale is associated with public

OPPOSITE
Traditional built form
(Drawings: Reinhard Behrens)

89

Traditional dormers
(Drawings: Reinhard Behrens)

buildings, shops, hotels and the like, while farm buildings and factories are associated with vehicles, machines and processes of production or storage – they have what can be called machine scale. Although insignificant in size, a telephone kiosk can look very conspicuous alongside a large factory building because of the scale relationship. Thus, problems of visual unity will arise when buildings of different scale-types appear together, and clear design guidelines need to be laid down for such mixed development.

The almost universal use of stone for external walls in traditional buildings has provided visual consistency in the past. Its use influenced the size and proportion of doors and windows, and led to façades with large expanses of solid wall pierced by relatively small windows with a vertical emphasis. There was a consistency in style between dwellings and other buildings, the width of roof spans being restricted by construction techniques so that even large buildings had well-proportioned pitched roofs, while the design of features such as dormers and upper loading doors also reflected domestic styles. There are also historical examples of timber and corrugated-iron buildings that integrate well with their local context, being sympathetic to the mainstream of stone buildings because of their compatible architectural form.

The farm steadings built in large numbers during the 18th and 19th centuries had a strong element of formality in their layout and architectural treatment. The principal façade was often symmetrically arranged around the courtyard entrance in the manner of Palladio, and this clearly expressed the point of access. A strong horizontal emphasis was created by an elongated form with simple façades and a gently punctuated roofline. In design, these steadings conform with the principles set out in this book, and the buildings were consequently well integrated into their landscape setting. For modern development in the countryside, the traditional farm steading is a good model to follow and could yield an improved architectural style and eliminate the random scatter of poorly integrated units that is so common today.

Within villages and small towns of the same period, traditional buildings were of a similar pattern to the farm steading. Well-tried principles of location and setting were followed, the layout was functional and individual buildings were usually unified by the use of similar materials and architectural styles. Buildings were aligned close to the edge of the pavement so that all private and garden space was located behind the house. This was normally surrounded by a high stone wall to provide enclosure and shelter, while public spaces were also well defined by this alignment of buildings and boundary walls. Later, buildings were set back to allow for a small front garden. Although there are notable exceptions, the streets were generally narrow, linked at right angles with pedestrian pends or closes to give a tightly-knit built environment that provided maximum shelter.

These traditional settlements grew gradually, without disrupting their established character because the same type of materials and built form were used, and each new addition adhered to the same pattern of layout. There was a clear distinction between private and public space, and points of access were located so that they could easily be seen. Although previous architectural styles were not always repeated, the overall impression was one of cohesion and unity (see p 119). Unfortunately, however, there are many recent examples of these principles having been ignored, with disastrous results for some attractive villages and small towns.

Culross Town House
(© *National Trust for Scotland*)

When things go wrong and how they can be put right. Good-looking buildings are all too frequently extended in the manner of this cottage at Clonyard Farm near Dalbeattie in Galloway, breaking all rules of good design (top). It has been remodelled by Benjamin Tindall for the new owner with a timber frame construction and harled external skin, using traditional dormers and windows with raised margins (bottom)

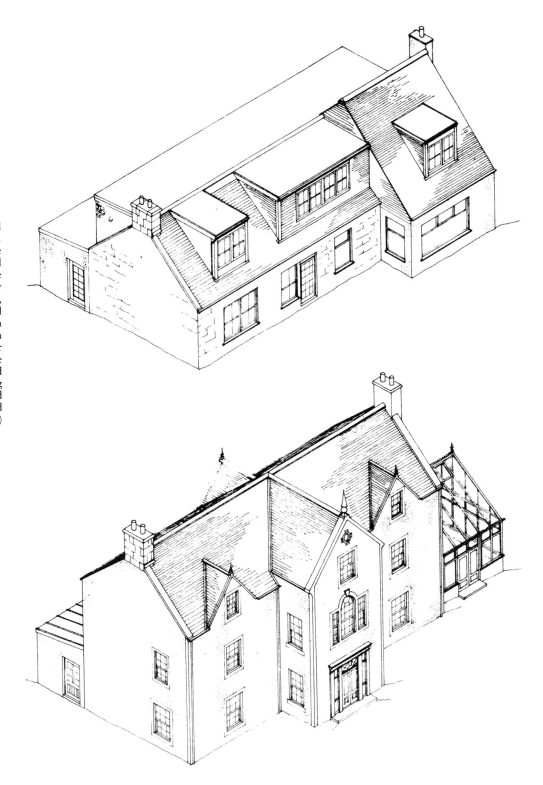

ADAPTING FOR NEW USES

If an existing building is to be adapted or extended to meet modern requirements, it is essential that the integrity of its external appearance is not destroyed. The same, or compatible, materials should be used and new door and window openings should be of the same proportions, their position not disrupting the pattern of elements on the façade. It is important that extensions for additional accommodation are executed in the same architectural style as the original building. In a case where the building is listed or located within a conservation area, special rules may apply in regard to details such as the choice of colour for external paintwork, and the maintenance of gutters and eaves and external rainwater pipes. Farm diversification and economic pressures on farming have made many farm steadings redundant for agricultural purposes, and there have been some very successful conversions for small-scale industries, craft enterprises and housing.

As well as the more obvious functional objectives, improvements are often made in the belief that additional accommodation and modernisation will enhance the market value of a property, but such investment may prove difficult to recoup. Although a wide 'box' dormer to provide additional floor space in a single-storey cottage may be easy to build and practical, it is likely to be out of scale and will have an adverse effect on visual appearance

An extension should be consistent with the original in form, scale and style. Pindlers Croft is part restoration (near wing) and part new (far wing), by the Law & Dunbar-Nasmith Partnership. Local stone in the boundary wall enhances unity, ties the building to its site and makes an attractive entrance, in character with the Morayshire setting

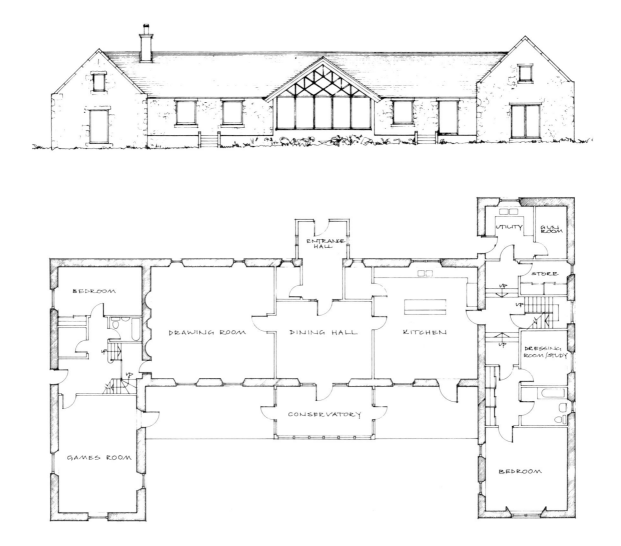

BEDROOM

DRAWING ROOM   DINING HALL   KITCHEN

ENTRANCE HALL

UTILITY   GUN ROOM

STORE

DRESSING ROOM / STUDY

CONSERVATORY

GAMES ROOM

BEDROOM

Design by Benjamin Tindall for the conversion of a redundant steading at Thistlecrook farm near Torphins in Kincardineshire to create one large dwelling that can easily be sub-divided into two units

(see p 118, bottom). The same applies when a large 'picture' window is introduced to replace traditional small windows, or when replacement windows in plastic or aluminium frames are installed (see p 18). The windows are the eyes of a building, being part of its beauty and character – this will be altered or destroyed like the human face should they be damaged.

A common addition is to build a garage, often awkwardly positioned in relation to the existing layout and invariably with a flat roof that is less effective and has a shorter life than a pitched one. Buyers of countryside properties are becoming more discerning, and the best way to ensure the enhanced resale value of a property is by respecting the architectural character of the original.

The best source of good practice in the restoration and adaptation of old buildings is the work of the National Trust for Scotland, under its Little

Houses Improvement Scheme. The sites where such schemes have been carried out, sometimes in collaboration with local councils, are well worth a visit and they set a standard which should be aimed at by all restorers of old properties. In addition, some local planning authorities have produced design guides to provide advice, some of which also apply to new buildings on vacant sites within a settlement. Unfortunately, few of these guides deal with landscape design, but they will generally be helpful in respect of the following elements:

- roof pitches
- chimney position
- treatment of gables and eaves
- fenestration pattern, including window and door surrounds
- dormers
- porches and extensions
- garages and outbuildings
- the cumulative effect of minor artefacts, for example vent pipes, television ariels and dishes, signs, solar panels and telephone and electricity connections
- the use of materials and colour

Such guidance documents should be consulted before planning any work of this type.

Architecture designed to enhance the countryside will look more appropriate, have a better relationship to its setting and produce more desirable places within which to live or work. It may also provide added value for owners and developers – an attractive building and site will generally be easier to sell and is likely to command a higher price. Those involved can gain satisfaction from creating something that will be an inspiration for future designers and a worthy contribution to our built heritage – a cultural heritage that is arguably being debased at present through ignorance of our inheritance and a lack of visionary creativity. In a recent commentary on the architectural sketchbooks of Sir Robert Lorimer, Charles McKean had this to say:

> Architecture is a cultural act. If a building is not created with cultural intent, it is not architecture. Yet the act of creation that underpins our architecture lies unacknowledged, misunderstood and undervalued.

FORM AND LAYOUT

1. Buildings and the layout of outdoor space should be designed as an entity and with simplicity.

2. Internal and external spaces should be designed so that their functions and relationships are easily perceived.

3. Design themes and functions of outdoor spaces should be kept to a minimum, including a clear distinction between private and public use.

4. Traditional pitched roofs have a longer life and look better than flat roofs.

5. The scale of a building should be appropriate for its use and relate to that of its neighbours.

6. The traditional farm steading is a good model to follow when arranging buildings to form enclosed space.

7. Built form and layout for extensions to settlements should respect existing character.

8. Extensions and modifications to existing buildings should respect existing style, detail and materials.

9. The windows are the eyes of a building and should be altered only as a last resort.

10. Countryside design should draw its inspiration from the locality rather than from models more suited to an urban context.

Topiary on a cottage wall in
Caithness. Planting to adorn
a building does not always
require a large site, but
originality and a sense of
humour are essential to
create this sort of
memorable effect (© *Scottish
Tourist Board*)

Upper gondola station and
restaurant at Aonach Mór
near Fort William, elevation
2,100 feet. Architects
Crerars & Partners, 1990
(Photo: Lorne Gill)

Buildings on mountains
where no trees will grow
present special difficulties of
visual intrusion, climatic
exposure and access.
Suitable siting, built form
and choice of colour are real
challenges for the designer

Ptarmigan observation
restaurant at the top of the
Cairngorm chairlift, near
Aviemore – a glazed drum
capped by a dome on
laminated timber supports,
elevation 3,600 feet.
Architects Magnus
Fladmark and Betty Moira
of Moira & Moira, 1966
*(Drawing: Reinhard Behrens,
Photo: Highlands & Islands
Enterprise)*

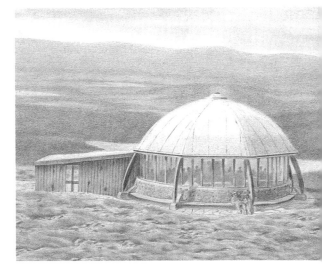

Woodland locations offer
shelter, and visual intrusion
is less of a problem, but
shadowing and moisture
from overhanging
vegetation are constraints

Rustic timber bothy near
Aberfeldy in Perthshire
(Photo: Lorne Gill)

Experimental design for a
walkers' bothy by Charles
Gulland under construction
in the grounds of Battleby
House near Perth, 1991
(Photo: Lorne Gill)

Pentland Hills Regional
Park, a well-designed visitor
centre appropriate for its use
and setting designed by Jim
Swanson of Lothian
Regional Council *(Photo:
John Foster)*

Talla Linfoots, where
boundary walls and
planting have been used to
modify the micro-climate
for livestock and human
habitation on an exposed
farm in Peeblesshire *(Photo:
Lorne Gill)*

Location of crofting settlements in the landscape of Vaternish at Lusta on Skye, looking across Loch Dunvegan *(Photo: Lorne Gill)*

Undulating landscape of small scale at Duirnish. Visual intrusion is minimised by siting on low ground for shelter. The buildings are aligned parallel with the contours and stepped down the slope, except for the new house in the background which is raised on an artificial platform *(Photo: Lorne Gill)*

Little Sparta at Dunsyre in Lanarkshire, water enhancing the setting of a building in the garden created by Ian Hamilton Finlay and his wife at Stonypath (© *Antonia Reeve Photography*)

The ornamental pond at Kelburn as it looks today (© *Earl of Glasgow*)

SCOTS PINE

BEECH

ELDER

HAWTHORNE

GOAT WILLOW

ELDER

ROWA

OAK

BEECH

APPLE

CHERRY

ALDER

YELLOW ASH

SILVER BIRCH

HOLLY

YEW

WALNUT

YEW

HAWTHORNE

Trees should be chosen according to the space available and the effect desired, having regard to the fact that each species grows at a different rate and reaches a different height when mature *(Drawing: Reinhard Behrens)*

Our inheritance of formally laid-out landscapes around buildings, as illustrated in James Proudfoot's drawing of the stand of Dobbies and the National Trust for Scotland at the Glasgow Garden Festival in 1988, by Catherine Orr of James Cunning Young & Partners (© *National Trust for Scotland*)

ETCH FROM NORTH WEST

The 'introverted' enclosure of the courtyard created by Sir Robert Lorimer on the north side of Formakin House as shown in his own sketch. The other perspective is of the south side which has an 'extroverted' garden with open views extending out into the surrounding countryside *(Drawings: The Formakin Trust)*

SKETCH FROM SOUTH WEST

Simplicity and clarity of
visual effects in built form
and layout were virtues
practised at Hill of Tarvit in
Fife by Sir Robert Lorimer,
the building and its
landscape setting being
locked together around a
strong central axis
(© *National Trust for Scotland*)

South Dell on Lewis, a linear crofting township set in an undulating and treeless landscape *(Photo: Patricia and Angus Macdonald)*

OPPOSITE
Arnol on Lewis, showing the successive phases of development in a crofting township *(Photo: Patricia and Angus Macdonald)*

Crail in Fife, showing the separation of public and private space in a traditional burgh, and the formation of terraces on sloping ground *(Photo: Patricia and Angus Macdonald)*

Traditional built form

Kellie Lodgings, Pittenweem *(© National Trust for Scotland)*

The Study, Culross
(© National Trust for Scotland)

Fenwick Church, Ayrshire
(Photo: Ken Andrew)

Compatibility of stone and
corrugated iron in two
adjacent cottages at Elphin
in Assynt *(Photo: Patricia and
Angus Macdonald)*

New box dormer on the left,
compared to the traditional
design on the right *(Photo:
Lorne Gill)*

Successive phases of development in the Fife village of Falkland. Each is of different architectural treatment, yet the overall impression is of cohesion and unity due to respect for the basic pattern of building line, height, roof shape and materials *(Photo: Lorne Gill)*

The Little Houses
Improvement Scheme,
operated by the National
Trust for Scotland, has set a
high standard for
rehabilitation and
conservation of old
buildings *(Photos: National
Trust for Scotland)*

Pan Ha', Dysart

The Anchorage, Dysart

West Shore, St Monans

OPPOSITE
Cobbled street, Dysart

Culross Abbey House,
based on John Slezer's
engraving of 1693, showing
the gardens laid out by Sir
Alexander Bruce and his
Dutch wife. The style is in
the formal renaissance
manner, yet irregular in its
adjustment to the site, the
landscaping almost taking
precedence over the
architecture

123

Buildings look more stable
and less conspicuous if the
roof is darker than the walls,
as on this farm in Glenshee
(Photo: Lorne Gill)

Landscape on Eigg in winter
snow (© *Highlands & Islands*
Enterprise)

Vernacular use of colour in
buildings

Tolsta, Lewis *(© Scottish
Tourist Board)*

Tobermory, Isle of Mull

Black Isle, Ross and
Cromarty

CHAPTER FIVE
COLOUR AND MATERIALS

This chapter is concerned with two further aspects of design which are of prime importance in ensuring that a building will harmonise with its surroundings. It is not enough to achieve good siting, built form and layout. The correct choice of colour and materials is essential if new development in the countryside is to be entirely successful in appearance. Historical examples of colours applied to buildings all over Britain can be found in *Your House* by John Prizeman, recommended as a good supplementary introduction to the subject, while *Theory and Use of Colour* by Lugina de Grandis is helpful on perception and colours in the landscape.

PERCEPTION OF COLOUR

In order to understand the significance of colour, it is helpful to know something about how colour is perceived and how that perception can be affected by different factors. What is loosely referred to as colour is defined by 'hue', 'luminosity' and 'chroma'. Hue is a single colour such as red, green or blue, the spectrum of hues normally being arranged in a circle for analytical purposes. Luminosity refers to the quality of lightness or darkness in a hue. Yellow appears the lightest because it is nearest to white, violet the least so because it is nearest to black. The descending scale of luminosity is yellow, orange, red and green equally, blue and then violet. Chroma is the purity or amount of pigment in a hue, the tonal value on the chromatic scale being determined by the amount of white or black added. White, black and grey are regarded as achromatic or neutral. Pairs of hues opposite each other in the colour circle are said to be complementary, as with green and red, which is why the barns of Norway and pantiled roofs in Scotland look so well in the countryside: when mixed in equal parts, complementary hues neutralise each other by turning into a greyish black.

For obvious reasons, it is the range of warm and golden hues known as 'earth colours' that is prevalent in the countryside. The three basic earths are obtained from secondary colours – dark red (violet+orange), yellow ochre (orange+green) and olive green (green+violet) – each tending towards the common primary of red, yellow and blue respectively. Clearly, the use of these earth colours on buildings in the countryside will best complement the natural environment throughout the seasons.

Warm colours are those associated with sunlight and fire, such as reds

OPPOSITE
Autumn colours at
Killiecrankie in Strathtay
(*Photo: Lorne Gill*)

129

and yellows, and most hues can be made warmer by adding to them a little of these colours. Association with water and sky makes blue appear cool. A warm light colour tends to advance and expand, while a cold, dark colour tends to retreat and contract. A certain weight can also be attributed to colours, yellow appearing the lightest and violet the heaviest in the chromatic circle.

People with normal sight see the same colour, but perceived intensity of chromatic tone or luminosity can be affected by factors such as age, knowledge, past associations and experience. The eye tires when it looks at one colour for more than 30 seconds, and fatigue varies according to the colour perceived, red causing the most rapid fatigue and blue the least. Adjoining colours will affect each other. For example, grey will seem greenish next to red, and reddish next to green. The eye will also accentuate differences – for example, green surrounded by yellow will appear cooler than the same green surrounded by blue. A large area of bright colour will swamp a small area of dull colour: conversely, a small area of bright colour will be accentuated in a large dull area. Moreover, distance and humidity are also significant factors. There will be a progressive loss of chromatic tonality with increased distance, and visibility is best when the air is dry.

COLOUR IN THE LANDSCAPE

Scotland's rapidly changing weather systems provide a seemingly infinite colour range of browns, greens, blues, purples and greys. But this palette is not static and the dynamics of seasonal change are an important consideration in the choice of colour for buildings. Changes throughout the year are represented by white blossoms, vibrant yellow gorse, bright-green foliage and new grasses in spring; a brief burst of early summer colours on farmed land; ripening crops below purple hills and the strong yellows and browns of bracken and deciduous woodlands in autumn; bluish-grey water when the days are short; and the whiteness of snow over browns and greens in winter. The strength and main direction of sunlight is also an important aspect of site assessment. For example, low winter sun will seem to intensify colour, whilst in bright summer light, colours will appear less strong.

The predominance of particular colours in a landscape is influenced by topography and the presence of water. The large expanse of blues and greys in the sea and sky accentuate the chromatic tonality of the greens and browns of the land in coastal areas, the sea and sky appearing lighter and the colours of the land darker in the evenings. In flat mainland landscapes the colour of the sky will dominate in a similar manner as on the coast and on islands but to a lesser extent, while in a hilly or mountainous area the colour of the land will dominate and shadowing will be an important factor to consider.

Colour in the landscape is also influenced by land use. Grazing by sheep and red deer has led to extensive areas of bare upland country with trees and shrubs confined to inaccessible places only. Thus, the land has a grassy smoothness with soft colours that merge into each other to produce a strong sense of unity. In the crofting counties this picture extends to include the farmed areas which are mostly under grass crops, and pastures with gentle variations in colour. Built development and roads in such a landscape have an immediate and strong impact caused by scars in the vegetation and the bright colours of new materials. In contrast, Lowland farming has produced landscapes with a more marked difference between cultivated and uncultivated land. There is a pronounced transition from the greens, yellow-browns or purples of pasture and bare upland moor, through to wooded headlands and cultivated fields with the strong and often contrasting colours of different crops – the strident yellow of rape has introduced a new colour dimension to such areas in recent years. In the Lowlands there is more woodland cover to ameliorate the impact of physical development, but the same care needs to be taken in the choice of colours for buildings.

COLOUR AND TEXTURE OF MATERIALS

Colour is a significant aspect of design due to its crucial effect on the visual perception of a building. The properties of a particular colour, as seen against a background of land, sea and sky, can be used to create both contrast and congruity. Light and bright colours should be chosen when the intention is to make a building appear closer, larger and more conspicuous, while dark or dull colours will help to reduce its impact on the surroundings. A roof will tend to reflect more light than the walls and the choice of roof colour is of key importance in reducing visual impact. Since dark or dull objects appear less obvious by tending to recede, a roof so coloured helps to anchor a building to its site. It is important that when a new building forms part of a settlement or a group, its roof colour matches that of neighbouring buildings as closely as possible.

For external walls without an applied finish, the different colours of local stone give variety to building character and enhance the sense of place in vernacular architecture. Sometimes the same stone was used for the whole building, while at other times contrasting sandstone was used for quoins at the corners and to form window and door surrounds. The main wall area in local stone provided unity, and the sandstone emphasised overall shape and punctuated the pattern of openings in a façade.

A lime-based wash was the traditional means of giving a building external colour, although the primary purpose of this treatment was to provide additional protection against rain. Without added pigment, this rendering is pure white and is mainly associated with the western parts of the country and the islands. In some areas pigments were added to the lime wash to produce ochre, pink and various pastel colours, and different binding agents were used as far back as medieval times to produce paint. The advent of cheap and widely available oil-based paint in the 19th century greatly enhanced the choice of colour: as with different stone types, one colour was used for the walls and another for picking out the margins of doors and windows.

An applied finish that is regarded as typically Scottish is wet-dash harling or rough cast, which provides an outer coating to stop water penetration and gives an appearance of unity. Paint can be applied to the harled surface or a pigment can be added to the mix to give a very durable colour finish, but alternatively, a dry-dash of fine gravel or broken seashells can be applied to the surface while the mix is still wet. This technique is known as 'pebble dash' and can give an attractive appearance when materials of local colour are used, although imported ingredients of the wrong colour can easily spoil the effect. The custom in the past was to apply these finishes down to ground level so that a building visually adhered to its site. The modern practice of terminating the harl at an exposed horizontal base course should be avoided as it gives the impression that the building is divorced from the ground on which it stands.

Vernacular use of colour in paintwork can be eccentric but is seldom dull, and the charm of many rural settlements can be attributed to this unpredictable diversity. The reason is often simply a matter of economy, like in coastal communities, where leftovers from boat painting are kept for decorating the house. In parts where corrugated iron is common for roofing, contrasting colours are often used for walls and roofs, and trims like bargeboards, ridge plates, window surrounds and porches are picked out in different colours. Although this invariably runs contrary to the rules of recommended practice, the perceived effect is of vitality and a strong sense of place. Among many others, Tobermory is a good example illustrating that there is no need to be afraid of the bold use of colour (see p 127).

Companies sometimes require that their corporate colours are applied to buildings and great care is then needed to avoid creating disharmony. For example, there is a temptation for commercial tourist developments to be painted in bright colours to attract attention, but this can be intrusive and counter-productive if insensitively handled. It is advisable to use earth colours associated with traditional and natural materials which blend best with those in the countryside, along with the dark grey of slate. A general rule, when in doubt, is to use a dark-colour option.

The basic procedure for colour selection is to prepare a colour chart of the main hues of vegetation etc. to appear on a site and its immediate surroundings, including the seasonal variations throughout the year, and use this as a guide to the most appropriate choices. It should be remembered that some local planning authorities recommend, or even specify, the range of colours which are considered appropriate for certain areas.

Another important influence on the appearance of a building is the texture of the building materials used. Texture relates to the unevenness of a surface, and is accentuated by the play of light and shadow. Different materials have different textures – a fine, smooth surface has a high reflectivity, while a coarse surface absorbs light and therefore appears darker. Textural effects can be created by the arranged juxtaposition of materials with contrasting textures. Texture can also be modified – for example, harling is finer than the coarse random rubble wall which it covers, and reflective surfaces can be dulled by painting.

However, texture and colour are equally important when choosing surface materials for spaces around a building. If the building is covered in pebble dash, slabs or gravel for paths and patio surfaces should have the same texture and colour to achieve unity. Similarly, these choices are also important for plant material. Cut grass gives a fine, smooth texture while shrubs and trees have volume and an uneven, coarser texture to contrast with smooth wall finishes. The permutations of texture and colour combinations are infinite.

USE OF MATERIALS

The geological processes that created Scotland's varied landscapes also provided stone as the common source of building material. Prior to the 20th century most buildings were erected in stone found locally: flagstone in Caithness and Orkney; whinstone in parts of the Borders, the Lothians, Fife, Stirlingshire, the south-west and in some of the Western Isles; and granite in Aberdeenshire and elsewhere in the south-west. However, the most common stone used in Scotland is sandstone in its many colours, while slate is the traditional roofing material.

The consistent use of stone over several centuries has given Scottish architecture its unity and strong visual character, despite changing styles of layout, form and ornamentation. Traditional stone walls were thick to assist stability, keep out the driving rain and act as a thermal reservoir, while coping stones to wall-heads and chimneys had generous overhangs to avoid water saturation and frost damage. But there were defects. Few buildings had a damp-proof course and the lower portions of walls were frequently wet, causing thermal loss and discomfort. Floor, roof and lintel timbers were frequently built into walls, resulting in subsequent decay, and pitched roofs often terminated in a raised coping wall or 'crow-stepped' gables with difficult and sometimes ineffective waterproofing. This was a hangover from the thatched roof that required end protection in a severe climate, but the technique continued in use after the introduction of slates, when it became a device to prevent the vulnerable slate eaves being lifted and blown off by wind.

The use of reconstituted stone blocks is becoming increasingly common both for main walls and in decorative panels associated with windows and doorways, but it is too seldom entirely successful. Despite advances in man-made materials, neither in initial appearance nor in weathering can they compete with natural stone. The use of many different materials will have a disruptive effect on visual unity and the best rule is to use as few as possible. Although to cover up the basic building material is not always appropriate, it is the use of wet-dash harl that gives so much of traditional Scottish architecture its strong sculptural effect and simple elegance.

When it comes to roofing, recycled slates from demolished buildings are now difficult to obtain, but quarries are being reopened and imported varieties are available. Pantiles of fired clay were traditional in many parts and are now manufactured, but a range of concrete tiles is also available and can be an acceptable alternative to both slates and clay tiles as long as an appropriate size and thickness is used and they are correctly coursed. The scale of roofing materials can be critical to the final appearance – many manufactured materials are inappropriately sized for domestic work in the countryside.

Corrugated-iron roofing has had a wide and long application in many parts. Leaving it to rust can remove reflectivity and create interesting colours, but this gives an impression of dereliction and it should either be painted or, alternatively, a pre-coated material should be used. Modern sheet metals can be very suitable if well detailed, but careful attention must be given to the surface profile so that the desired textural effect is obtained.

The use of brick construction in Scotland goes back almost 200 years, but it has played only a minor part until recently. Its main application was for industrial buildings, and many fine examples of patterned brickwork can still be seen in urban areas. It was often used in association with stone, either as the main material, or for detailing of quoins at corners and openings, and for arches and lintels – a recent example of this being Steedman's house at Muir of Blebo in Fife (see pp 154–5).

Although wood was not widely used, there are surviving examples of Victorian and Edwardian timber buildings (see p 148). Corrugated-iron was also used during this period in a wide range of prefabricated buildings – referred to by Edwin Johnston as the 'tin tradition' (see pp 149–51). Several types seem to have been specially designed for their locations, using standard components in shape and form which fitted well into a country-side setting. However, many catalogues illustrated designs of bungalows, shooting lodges, schools and churches which were thought to be just as appropriate for use overseas in the colonies as in this country.

Wood is a natural material and the traditional designs of a hundred years ago show that timber buildings can be given an architectural form which links well with stone buildings (see p 151). The same applies to timber dwellings imported from Scandinavia and to a wide range of buildings used by the Forestry Commission. A key principle is that the building should be predominantly in timber, with consistently applied external construction details. Boarding of straight edges and wide dimensions will usually look best, as it will be in scale with both the building and its surroundings. A variety of roof-cladding materials can be considered, depending upon the context of the site.

Timber can also be used for entrance porches and extensions to stone buildings, but panels with narrow boards or small areas of wood tend to look fussy and out of proportion. Insufficient attention has been paid to the visual effects of how timber boards are aligned, whether in a vertical or horizontal format. The vertical option is usually most satisfactory if timber is the main cladding material, but in circumstances where horizontal boarding is required, it should be fixed with staggered joints like dressed masonry or, alternatively, covered joints should fall on structural members to form panels.

The integration of stone and timber buildings within the same group presents special difficulties because of the difference in appearance and properties of each material. In a stone building the walls tend to dominate architectural form, while in a timber building the roof tends to dominate. There are several reasons for this. Timber buildings tend to have overhanging eaves which form shadow and thereby appear closer to the ground, while the larger roof area also reflects more light and makes it appear more dominant. Stone has a more solid feel than timber and there is a stronger difference between solid walls and voids for doors and windows. There is also the fact that the gable walls have traditionally terminated above the roof, giving a smaller roof area, especially with the eaves flush with the wall at the gutter. Although many Victorian and Edwardian architects knew how to achieve compatibility whether they used stone, brick or timber, the secret seems to have eluded British designers in more recent times.

Whenever possible, boundary walls should be constructed in natural stone, preferably using a local style of construction. The height of a wall and its angle should follow the gradient of the ground level and not be stepped in the manner of modern brick walls which are constructed with horizontal courses. If block-work has to be used, a well keyed and bonded harl or lime wash should be applied, the top of the wall always being angled according to the ground gradient. A top coping in local stone greatly enhances the visual effect.

Patio surfaces should be made from slabs with a texture and in a colour consistent with adjoining materials. When tarmacadam is used, the colour of aggregate or gravel for top dressing should be carefully chosen to

Too many different materials give a fussy appearance, as in this modern bungalow before treatment (top). This can be overcome by removing the timber cladding and extending the harled finish to cover all wall surfaces, including areas of exposed masonry. Enclosing the cut-away corner at the entrance will provide more indoor space and achieve a more balanced gable elevation. Pitched roofs on the dormer and the garage will make the whole composition more consistent in style, and more suitable windows will further enhance appearance – as will modification to the stepped boundary wall (bottom) *(Drawings: Reinhard Behrens)*

harmonise with the surroundings. Concrete kerbing and the use of paving blocks are more suited to urban and industrial areas than rural areas and should be avoided. A range of materials can be used for paths, but the same rules apply in the use of colour and edging. Where traditional and modern materials are of broadly similar costs, the former is recommended and, whilst many modern materials can be used as appropriate substitutes, they must be compatible in colour and texture with the local context. However, there is a risk that modern materials will not weather well – few manufactured materials can match natural materials for their mature appearance after a few years.

A further consideration in the use of materials is the maintenance implication for the expected life of a development. Not only should materials be chosen for their maintenance and weathering characteristics, but the regime of maintenance itself should be appropriate to a rural situation. Early consideration of this issue usually leads to significant economies and a much more acceptable appearance, so the design team should work out and cost management regimes for buildings, hard ground surfaces, trees and shrubs, all types of soft ground cover and for any water bodies forming part of a proposed development.

For certain types of present-day buildings, using modern materials that are maintenance free within their relatively short lifespan, the issue arises of what will last longer – the designed landscape or the buildings. The life expectancy of a maintenance-free and disposable architecture is set by investment criteria that are relatively short-term. In contrast, the lifespan of certain species of trees extends over several hundred years before they reach full maturity. This touches on the timeless quality of historic architecture, often attributable to its mature landscape setting, and there is a need to consider site planting for modern development as a relatively permanent setting for several generations of buildings. There are the Cadzow Oaks from the 15th century, and the Fortingall Yew is an extreme example of a tree that has survived for more than 3,000 years.

Walter Gropius observed that 'there is no finality in architecture, only continuous change'. This touches on the concepts of beauty and fashion – neither of which is static. Since the appearance of buildings tends to reflect prevailing fashion, this presents less of a problem in an urban context than in the countryside, where the designer has to work in harmony with the natural order. In a riposte to the Gropius-type assertion, Haythornthwaite has explained it like this:

> When man enters upon the natural scene and modifies its vegetation, domesticates animals or erects buildings, he does not necessarily depart from the natural order of which he himself is a part. If he confines his economy to the materials available within the locality and responds to the natural conditions of the locality, its climate, the levels of the land, constituents of the soils, this merely emphasises the characteristics of the locality and adds a human element to the sum of natural beauty, which is unchanging.

This is the reason why the basic architectural form of buildings appearing in the countryside today is still essentially the same as that of the Stone Age timber hall of Balbridie on Deeside, built over 5,000 years ago, in the same country, in the same climate and for the same purpose – to provide human shelter (see p 17).

COLOUR AND MATERIALS

1. Earth colours will best complement the natural environment throughout the seasons in the countryside.

2. Bright colours appear to advance and expand, while dark colours appear to retreat and contract.

3. Buildings look more stable and less conspicuous if the roof is darker than the walls.

4. Contrasting colours can be used selectively to emphasise certain elements of a building.

5. The same colour can be used to unify a group of disparate buildings, while different colours can be used to break down a building of large bulk.

6. Materials should be appropriate for the climate, ecology, texture and scale of the site and should be capable of weathering well over time.

7. Traditional materials should be used where possible, particularly near existing buildings.

8. The use of many different materials in a building will have a disruptive effect on visual unity.

9. The built environment is static with intermittent maintenance requirements, while landscape elements change with the seasons and over time and demand frequent maintenance.

CHAPTER SIX

TOMORROW'S HERITAGE

This chapter traces the evolution of ideas that have set the trends in architecture and landscape design over the last hundred years. By way of example it refers to Lorimer and Mackintosh – designers who believed that the source of a nation's true architecture is derived from its historical roots, but who were also among the first Scottish architects to break away from the old order by acknowledging the need to embrace new design ideas. Their work signalled the shape of things to come, and was much in tune with the pace of technological and social change that followed in the 1930s and found architectural expression in the Modern Movement. A brief analysis of the Scottish response to modernism follows, with selected examples of good practice from the last 30 years to illustrate how the principles set out in this book are being applied by modern designers to create tomorrow's heritage.

CONTEXTUAL BEGINNINGS

The antecedents of modernism go back to the Gothic revival in the second half of the last century. A renewed interest in traditional arts and crafts was kindled by a response to the rigidity of classicism, together with a reaction to the Industrial Revolution. There was also a revival of the renaissance principle that house and garden were indivisible entities to be designed together. For this to happen successfully, both the architect and landscape designer had to work jointly. The long and well-documented partnership between architect Edwin Lutyens (1869–1944) and garden designer Gertrude Jekyll (1843–1932) was a source of inspiration for contemporaries as well as those who have subsequently sought to follow their example. This prolific pair worked mostly in England and it is believed that they came to Scotland only once – in 1901, to create The Greywalls in Gullane (see p 140). The formal layout is typical of Lutyens' work, and the house and garden come together in a masterful arrangement of spaces formed by stone walls that connect with the main building to create a feeling of unity. He also succeeded in giving The Greywalls a Scottish character, which speaks for his understanding of place and cultural context.

By the turn of the century the Arts and Crafts Movement had become an influential force, Sir Robert Lorimer (1864–1929) being the best known architect associated with its foothold in Scotland. Although mostly remembered for the restoration of several well-known historic houses – including the family home at Kellie Castle in Fife – he was in his own time regarded as a progressive architect. He designed a great variety of buildings for countryside settings, introducing a strong vernacular flavour in a modern style, best exemplified by a series of houses built in Colinton (see p 143), at that time a small village reached by railway from Edinburgh. His greatest contribution to modern architecture, however, was to bring landscape and buildings together in a unified design. He met and was influenced by Gertrude Jekyll, and her feeling for plants and their arrangement can be seen in many Lorimer projects. He too relied on the use of walls to create space, define lines of movement and help tie a development together (see p 65). Like Jekyll, he sought to combine the formal and the picturesque, skilfully exemplified in his design for the house and garden at Formakin – on one side the open parkland runs right up to the walls of the house, and on the other, walls extend outwards to provide an enclosed garden space (see pp 112–3) – design techniques referred to by Sylvia Crowe as means of creating 'extroverted' and 'introverted' spaces.

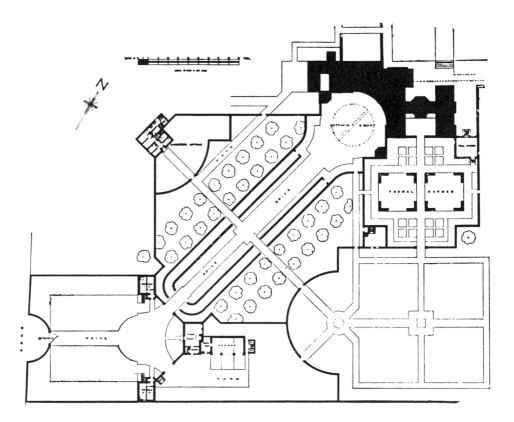

The plan of Greywalls in Gullane, by Edwin Lutyens, 1901

Charles Rennie Mackintosh (1868–1928) was equally rooted in the 'native' architecture of Scotland, but his receipt of The Alexander Thomson Studentship in 1886 offered an early opportunity for travel abroad and he later became associated with the Art Nouveau style and developed a more overtly modern approach to design, his thinking having been inspired by ideas acquired when working in Europe. Few of his designs were built, but examples at Windyhill in Kilmacolm (see pp 162–3) and Hill House in Helensburgh (see pp 10 and 164), rather like his paintings, show a great feeling for landscape. He took great care over layout and outdoor spaces, as confirmed by one of his biographers, Thomas Howarth, who says:

> Mackintosh always paid close attention to siting, orientation and layout; his houses seem to form part of the landscape, they grow from the soil and at Hill House in particular, the garden was arranged to the architect's instructions in order to enhance the long sweeping lines of the principal façade. At Windyhill, built on a precipitous open site, he used garden furniture and openwork screens to help unite man-made and natural elements.

Two of the most influential pioneers of modern architecture, Frank Lloyd Wright (1869–1959) in America and Le Corbusier (1887–1965) in France, both had a strong interest in the relationship between architecture and landscape. Le Corbusier had an early preoccupation with alpine architecture, and his first villa designs are interesting in their use of walls and terraced levels to fit buildings into steeply sloping sites. Wright, on the other hand, was essentially an architect of the countryside with a strong interest in craftsmanship, and his main contribution was to introduce the concept of 'organic' architecture, developed from a study of how to marry buildings with the shapes and materials of the site, so that in some of his designs it is difficult to discern where the site ends and the building begins. Nikolaus Pevsner speaks of his approach as 'a vision of the house embedded in its natural surroundings and opening towards them by means of terraces and cantilevered roofs'.

ARRIVAL OF MODERNISM

Charles McKean's recent book *The Scottish Thirties* gives a good account of the response by Scottish architects to international modernism. The use of harled brickwork or poured-concrete construction, combined with rectilinear shapes and flat roofs, were the functional manifestations of machine-age architecture. This new vision of simple cubist design was introduced to the broad mass of the Scottish people by the 1938 Empire Exhibition in Glasgow. Many public buildings, hotels, cinemas and factories of this time were built in the new style. Some blocks of flats were also built, but there was only a limited demand for the modern style in

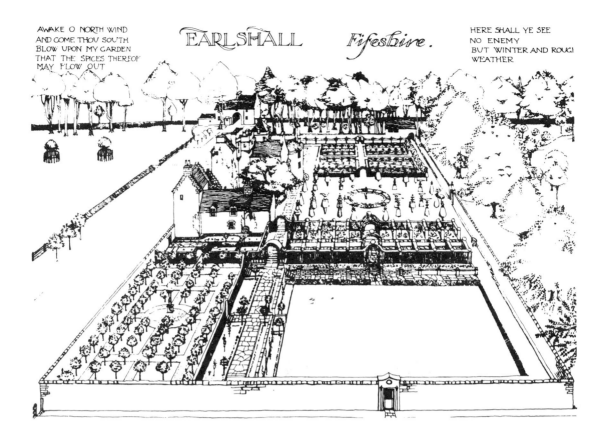

AWAKE O NORTH WIND
AND COME THOU SOUTH
BLOW UPON MY GARDEN
THAT THE SPICES THEREOF
MAY FLOW OUT

EARLSHALL   *Fifeshire.*

HERE SHALL YE SEE
NO ENEMY
BUT WINTER AND ROUGH
WEATHER

Lorimer also designed timber houses built in Scandinavia. At the turn of the century he was commissioned to design a summer house for Lord Salvesen in a woodland setting outside Mandal in Southern Norway
(Photo: Sir Maxwell Harper Gow)

Earlshall in Fife was Robert Lorimer's first restoration project, 1891–94. As in all his other work, the gardens at Earlshall were given as much attention as the buildings. The drawing by H. I. Triggs, dated 1900, shows how the Lorimer design was implemented with small outdoor rooms next to the house that lead to larger courtyards enclosed by stone walls and hedges, the whole arrangement being linked by a system of paths and archways
(Trustees of the National Library of Scotland)

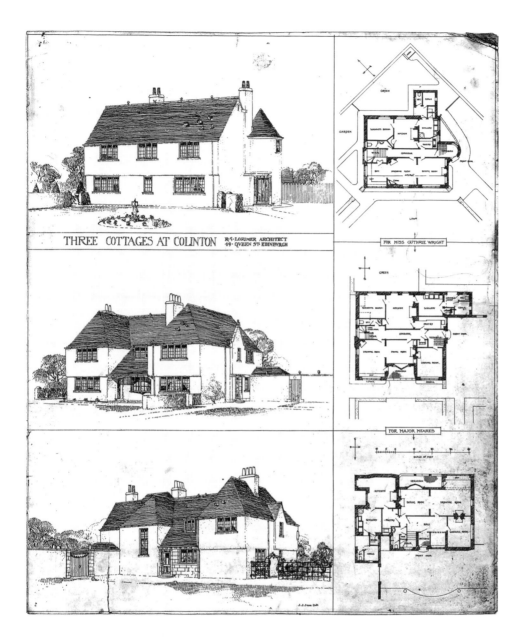

THREE COTTAGES AT COLINTON R·S·LORIMER ARCHITECT 49· QVEEN S⁺ʰ EDINBVRGH

FOR MISS GUTHRIE WRIGHT

FOR MAJOR MEARES

Drawings of the first Colinton cottages by Robert Lorimer were exhibited at the Royal Scottish Academy in 1896. They owe more to the style popular with followers of the arts and crafts movement in the South than to local Scottish tradition, except for the white harled walls and a touch of baronial in the circular stairtower. The eaves were kept low by just over-shooting the top of the first floor windows, two cottages have hipped gables, and he used pressed red clay tiles for the roofs
(© RCAHMS)

residential development, the majority of owners preferring the more traditional-looking bungalow.

Although the 1930s was an exciting period of experimentation with new ideas, there is little evidence that architects of this time sought to emulate the approach of Lorimer and Mackintosh, who designed the buildings together with their landscape setting. However, there were clearly different attitudes to rural development and some members of the profession were actively involved when the Association for the Preservation of Rural Scotland was established in 1926, partly as a reaction to the increasing urbanisation of the countryside. A key part of their campaign to improve rural design standards was to produce and promote, under the auspices of the Association, a set of standard house plans (see pp 166–7). This initiative had the blessing of Government, and the then Secretary of State for Scotland, the Rt Hon William Adamson, made this supportive statement at the Association's annual conference in 1931:

> I am pleased to know that the Association in co-operation with other public-spirited bodies are taking steps so that local authorities and private enterprise may have made available to them for a small fee alternative plans and elevations prepared by skilled architects. By adopting these plans, builders will have a guarantee that they are not building out of harmony with the traditions of Scottish domestic architecture. It is true that the Department of Health requires to keep a strict check on cost, but, as the Association realises, there is no necessary antagonism between good design and economy.

The new architecture inspired by the Modern Movement changed the look of buildings, but few architects seem to have been able to give the new style a distinctly Scottish face. The text of *Building Scotland* by Alan Reiach and Robert Hurd, published by the Saltire Society in 1941, bears this out. The authors dwell on the quality of Scottish landscapes and traditional architecture, speculate on the future by showing modern buildings in Scandinavia, Switzerland and Czechoslovakia, but stop short of offering design advice on the way forward – the dilemma of the 1930s being neatly encapsulated in the following assertion:

> Tradition is the pool of a nation's continued experience, from which we can draw both inspiration and warning. Slavish copying of period styles in buildings for modern needs produces dreary archaisms, but plan, form, proportion and colour of building in one country differs from those in another, and it would be foolish to ignore the social, physical and psychological reasons behind these national differences. Pioneer architect, Charles Rennie Mackintosh, whose influence on modern European design was considerable, himself drew inspiration direct from basic Scottish traditions . . . but he was a prophet in his own country.

After the disruption of World War II a new generation came on the scene to put the aspirations of Reiach and Hurd into practice, and the results were selectively reviewed by Peter Willis in *New Architecture in Scotland*. Among the young architects of the 1950s, he refers to the work of James Morris and Robert Steedman, providing a good example of how post-war modernism arrived in Scotland. After qualifying from Edinburgh College of Art they went to study landscape architecture at the University of Pennsylvania. Like other young Scots who followed the same academic route, they were able to travel and see the buildings designed by great names of modern architecture such as Frank Lloyd Wright, Mies van der Rohe,

OPPOSITE
Only masterful artistry and respect for vernacular simplicity can create the elegant interplay of materials, colour and decorative detailing achieved in this part elevation of an Inverness-shire cottage
(© *Scottish Tourist Board*)

Vernacular use of colour at
Plockton, Wester Ross
(© *Scottish Tourist Board*)

The colour of plants and
flowers artistically arranged
against a whitewashed
cottage wall in Moniaive,
Dumfriesshire (© *Scottish
Tourist Board*)

A rare Scottish example of
early brickwork in a
domestic building at
Flatfield Farm on the Carse
of Gowrie, Firth of Tay
(Photo: Ruth Grant)

The contrasting colour and
texture of a harled wall and
flowering shrubs at
Inverewe in Wester Ross
(Photo: Lorne Gill)

An attractive combination
of timber and whitewashed
brickwork in Almondbank,
Perthshire

Syre Church, Strathnaver
(© *Highlands & Islands Enterprise*)

Corrugated iron as an external cladding material has a long history, sometimes referred to as the 'tin tradition'. It produced an architecture of great charm and vigour, entirely compatible with its neighbours built in other materials. As the high-tech answers of a bygone era, these buildings hold valuable lessons for designers today

Croft houses, Skye

Bungalow, Barra

Croft house, Harris *(Photo: Thomas Huxley)*

A timber-framed cottage
with external cladding in
horizontal boarding at Loch
Alvie in Badenoch and
Strathspey *(Photo: Benjamin
Tindall)*

Village hall, Newtonmore
*(Photo: Patricia and Angus
Macdonald)*

Our architectural heritage at its best. Whitewashed harl unifies this group of buildings, and boundary walls in local stone tie them into their setting at Plockton in Wester Ross *(Photo: Lorne Gill)*

Muir of Blebo in Fife, by Robert Steedman, 1988. The building is sited along the contours, and the floor levels are related to the sloping ground by the main entrance being to the first floor from the upper part of the site and the ground-floor rooms opening on to the garden terrace below. The styling is truly modern inside and out, but the use of sandstone and brick arches makes the building belong to Fife *(© A. L. Hunter Photography)*

Housing at Bridgend on the banks of the River Tay below Kinnoull Hill in Perth, by Angus Macdonald and James Stephen of the Parr Partnership, 1975. Recipient of several national and international design awards, this development of 40 houses pioneered a fresh approach to making modern housing compatible with an historic setting. The creation of spaces and stepped terraces on a sloping site, together with sensitive planting designed by Derek Lovejoy of Perth, have resulted in a harmonious transition between the townscape and its wider landscape setting. The widely acclaimed success of the scheme was commemorated on a postage stamp to mark the Festival of Architecture in 1984

Residential development at St Magdalene's Distillery in Linlithgow, designed by Alfred Cooper, 1989 and being built by Laing Homes at the time of writing. The styling has a strong feel of Mackintosh, and the garages are built into the sloping site to achieve a well-integrated relationship between ground and floor levels *(Drawing: Gaynor Shepherd)*

The Earl's Gate residential development in the grounds of Aberdour House in Fife by Tulloch Homes, architectural design by McFarlane & Curran of Dunfermline and landscape design by Grazina Portal, 1991. It is remarkable for the good integration of layout, built form and landscape. *(Artwork: Dynam Graphics)*

Existing trees are a designer's greatest asset when planning a new development. Mature woodlands have been retained to enhance the setting for the pavilion at the West of Scotland Science Park on the banks of the River Kelvin at Maryhill. Architecture and landscape design by Gillespies

The British Golf Museum in St Andrews, by Larry Rolland of the Hurd Rolland Partnership with Andrew Merrylees, 1988. To avoid visual intrusion in a sensitive setting, the building has been dug into the site and the ground rolled back over the building to form a roof that is an extension of the surrounding landscape *(Photo: Bob Aird, Drawings: Nicholas Taylor)*

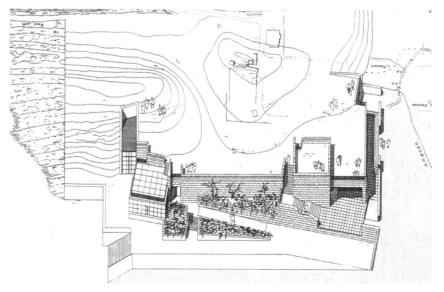

Richard Neutra and Marcel Breuer. Duly inspired by this new vision of architecture, they returned in 1957 to establish their Edinburgh practice, and through teaching influenced the next generation of students to recognise the interdependence of architecture and landscape design, and the idea of drawing inspiration from the site.

Their first house, designed for a flat and wooded site at Cramond (see p 169, top), features three characteristics typical of the Morris & Steedman approach to design. Its architectural form is strikingly modern, the use of local sandstone and high walls to create sheltered spaces is traditionally Scottish, and the building and its landscape setting have been designed as an integrated whole. Other examples of their work are houses in East Kilbride (see p 169, bottom), on the edge of the Pentland Hills (see pp 170–1) and Steedman's own house at Muir of Blebo in Fife (see pp 154–5). They have also shown that traditional buildings can be modified and extended in a manner that enhances rather than detracts from the original, as illustrated in their design for the conference centre of the Countryside Commission for Scotland at Battleby House near Perth. In recent years it is possible to discern a gradual evolution in their work from the very modernistic buildings of the 1960s to a more relaxed and truly Scottish style.

There were, of course, many other architects at this time who pursued a vigorous modernist style in their work, such as Robert, Matthew & Johnson-Marshall for the campus at Stirling University, James Stirling for his student residences at St Andrew's University, and Gillespie Kidd & Coia for St Peter's College in Cardross. Another was Peter Womersley whose uncompromisingly modern-looking but sensitively designed buildings were much admired, such as his Galashiels studio of 1972 for Bernat Klein. Respect for the setting of a building was one of his great virtues and the Klein studio adheres to the Morris & Steedman dictum that 'a building is easier to move than existing trees': the attractive Galashiels parkland setting remains virtually intact to enhance the concrete and glass structure. On the other hand, his ability to combine a truly modern style with elements of Scottishness was demonstrated in the 1967 consulting-rooms for a medical group practice on the outskirts of Kelso. On one occasion, when asked by a journalist to comment on the work of another architect – a controversial modern building in an historic setting – Womersley responded that an old building should never be demolished unless that replacing it was of a better design and of higher quality than the original.

POST-MODERNIST TRENDS

During the period of post-war reconstruction the architectural profession in Britain, both in practice and in the education of students, embraced modernism to the exclusion of almost all else. This trend was consolidated

Windyhill in Kilmacolm, by Charles Rennie Mackintosh, 1900. Mackintosh's holistic design approach to architecture and landscaping is revealed in his own drawings, showing a meticulous attention to the relationship between internal and external spaces, the positioning of trees and shrubs, and the use of levels and boundary walls to create outdoor rooms and thereby lock a building into its site:

Perspective from the north-east *(Coll: Glasgow School of Art)*

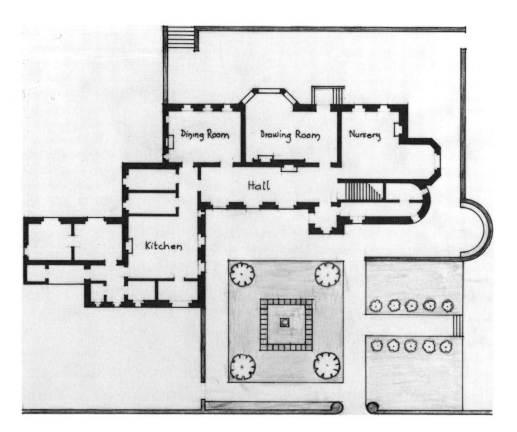

Floor plan and garden layout

Perspective from the
south-west *(Coll: Glasgow
School of Art)*

in the 1950s and '60s when the central areas of many cities were
comprehensively redeveloped and there was a boom in the construction of
public sector housing – including many high-rise tower blocks in the
countryside on the edge of towns. Although the public may not have been
much enamoured by the buildings in which they were expected to live and
work, few dared to question what was being put up, and there was little
encouragement for architects who were interested in the continuity of local
tradition and craft-based solutions. This gave modernist architecture a
monopoly that eventually made it as eclectic within a narrow range of
design solutions as 19th-century architecture had been narrow and eclectic
in its use of classical ornamentation. But in the last 15 years there has been a
sea change in attitude. Public criticism has become more assertive, people
are more discerning about what sort of built environment is desirable now
and for the future, and many more architects are seeking inspiration from a
broader base of ideas. This has led to a more pluralistic approach to design,
the previous 'monoculture' of modernism having been relegated to sit
alongside other stylistic trends based on classical or vernacular models.
Charles Jencks and other commentators who have written about these
recent trends refer to them collectively as 'post-modernism'.

Recent debate has been much enlivened by the strong views held, and
publicly expressed, by HRH The Prince of Wales. His 1987 speech to the
Royal Institute of British Architects at the Mansion House in London, in
which he criticised the profession's lack of respect for setting and cultural
context, was a turning point. The reaction of the Institute, on behalf of
architects in the south, has been rather hostile to such criticism. The Royal
Incorporation of Architects in Scotland, however, has responded more
positively by regarding such views as a welcome broadening of the debate
about the built environment – a debate further enlivened by the Prince's

subsequent television programme and book on the future of architecture.

In the introduction to their booklet *Scottish Architecture in the Nineteen Eighties* the Royal Incorporation of Architects in Scotland state that:

What has been built is so different from what would have been even ten years ago, that we are looking at the stirring of a new Scots architecture. The first element that strikes is the colour, accompanied by picturesque shapes: no more grey monoliths. It is either a response to the building's function or a response to its location. We now appreciate our vigorous Victorian legacy as much as we do that of earlier periods, and recognise the means by which the results were achieved. Massing, roofscape, craftsmanship and applied art seem set to make a come-back almost a hundred years after they burst upon the new streets of Glasgow, Edinburgh and Aberdeen. The source of inspiration is generally that of the building's immediate neighbours, tempered by the international trends within which we live. At the moment Scotland's modern architecture encompasses the entire spectrum from home-grown traditionalism to high-tech modernism.

Hill House in Helensburgh, by Charles Rennie Mackintosh, 1902. Perpective from the north-east *(Coll: Kenneth Lawson, Photo: Hunterian Art Gallery)*

These words reflect a new-found Scottish pride in local tradition, combined with an acceptance of present-day needs and technological opportunities, and what is encouraging about this new attitude is that the moral high ground is no longer held by followers of a single persuasion. It is again respectable to be interested in the conservation and rehabilitation of old properties and to be inspired by Scotland's local traditions. The more tolerant atmosphere, in which modernism is one style among equals, has been conducive to the re-examination of old values and the principles set out in this book. It has been particularly encouraging for young designers who see merit in a more integrated approach on the lines of Lorimer and Mackintosh, with a stronger emphasis on context.

This has made it possible for architects to acquire reputations and prosper on conservation work, thereby stimulating a revival in traditional arts and crafts skills. Among such architects are William Cadell of Linlithgow, Benjamin Tindall of Edinburgh, John Boys and Geoffrey Jarvis of Glasgow and James Simpson of Simpson & Brown, whose main preoccupation is to restore surviving William Adam buildings. Much of the credit for the rediscovery of traditional styles and design skills is due to the activities of bodies like the Architectural Heritage Society of Scotland and the Scottish Vernacular Buildings Working Group, as well as to the dedicated work of teachers like Colin McWilliam (1928–1989) whose academic career at Edinburgh College of Art was devoted to communicating the virtue of mixed development in which the best of the old is retained and the new is designed to respect its neighbours – the essence of sound contextual practice.

Good examples of the new pride in, and respect for, our architectural inheritance are Benjamin Tindall's conversion of a previously enlarged cottage into a family residence at Clonyard Farm in Galloway (see p 92) and in his design for turning a redundant farm steading into two modern dwellings at Thistlecrook Farm near Banchory (see p 94). The transfer of such skills to new development is shown in his design for a proposed Nordic Ski Centre at Aviemore that will have traditional timber walls and a corrugated-iron roof to echo the style of other buildings on the Rothiemurchus Estate. The adaptation of kit-houses to suit their setting is another challenge now being tackled by post-modernists, and Alasdair Alldridge's design for a new house at Ebort on Skye shows what can be achieved when the motivation is to develop an appropriate architecture for the countryside. Another skilful design illustrating what is possible with a modified kit is the house in St John's Town of Dalry by Antony Wolffe (see p 173).

Robert Hurd established an architectural practice in 1933, through which he sought to promote the ideas of Mackintosh for whom he had a high regard. Hurd was also against the dead hand of 19th-century eclecticism, and for him the Art Nouveau style embodied the progressive spirit of the 20th century. Now known as the Hurd Rolland Partnership, their headquarters are at Rossend Castle in Burntisland, and Larry Rolland and Ian Begg are well-known names associated with their more recent work. The practice has always taken as its starting point the setting into which a building has to be placed. In this respect, they talk about the surrounding landscape, materials and scale as constituting the 'language of setting'. The present partners still believe in the Hurd philosophy that the future comes from the past, and that good buildings emerge from the development of traditional qualities, as exemplified by their work at Kenmore in Strathtay (see pp 180–3).

The legacy of Hurd and Lorimer was also carried forward by Alan Reiach as mentioned above, who served his apprenticeship in Lorimer's office. He formed his first partnership with Professor Ralph Cowan in 1948, and both acquired an admiration for the work of Scandinavian architects like Gunnar Asplund, Arne Jacobsen and Alvar Alto, influential in Reiach's development of a modern style that can be traced into his later partnership with Stuart Renton and Eric Hall. Although located in an urban setting, the 1962 design by Reiach & Renton for Kildrum Parish Church at Cumbernauld (see p 177) is a delightful monument of Scottish modernism from this period. The style and architectural form are clearly inspired by

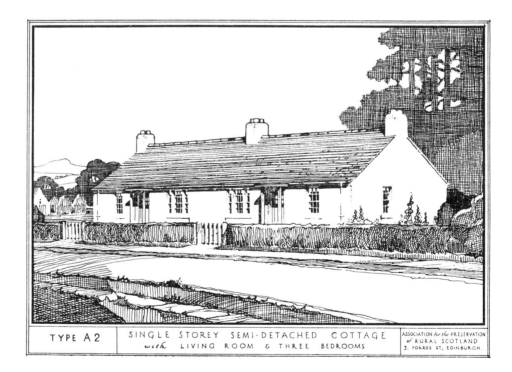

| TYPE A 2 | SINGLE STOREY SEMI-DETACHED COTTAGE with LIVING ROOM & THREE BEDROOMS | ASSOCIATION for the PRESERVATION of RURAL SCOTLAND 3. FORRES ST, EDINBURGH. |

Alto, but the layout of the courtyards and the landscape treatment of the setting would have been approved of by Hurd and Lorimer as suitably Scottish in character.

Among the practices which have consistently pursued a design philosophy in accordance with the principles advocated in this book is the Law & Dunbar-Nasmith Partnership, founded in 1957. As a student at Cambridge, Graham Law was encouraged by Professor Nikolaus Pevsner to study the work of Alexander 'Greek' Thomson, which became the subject of his degree dissertation and a lasting influence. The output of the partnership has been characterised by a sensitivity to place and local tradition in the spirit of Lutyens and Jekyll, and their approach to site analysis and visual impact has also been influenced by Le Corbusier's practice of sketching the horizons and making buildings become an echo of the landscape, the design for Pitlochry Festival Theatre being just such an example of a successful marriage between modern architecture and a sensitive setting (see p 179). Restoration and conversion work has included Fort George and the Maltings Art Centre in Berwick-upon-Tweed. They have designed many rural houses, including the Duke of York's residence at Sunninghill Park, Windsor and Pindlers Croft in Morayshire (see p 93), and they have in recent years undertaken an integrated programme of

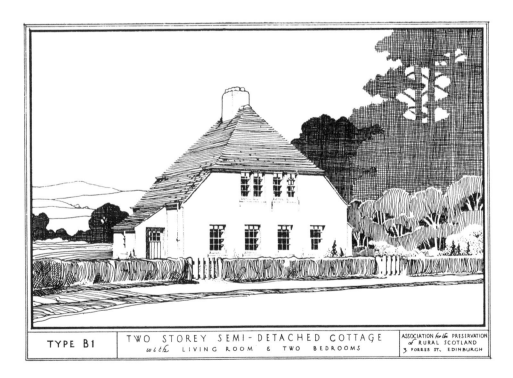

TYPE B1 — TWO STOREY SEMI-DETACHED COTTAGE with LIVING ROOM & TWO BEDROOMS

ASSOCIATION for the PRESERVATION of RURAL SCOTLAND
3, FORRES ST., EDINBURGH

Two house types designed by Sir Frank Mears and Leslie Graham Thomson at the request of the Association for the Protection of Rural Scotland. Sets of working drawings for these were on offer in 1932 to local authorities and private individuals at a price ranging from £1 per unit for schemes of more than 12 to £9 for a single house (© APRS)

conservation and new housing on the royal estate at Balmoral.

Another practice which regards landscape design as an integral part of architecture is the Parr Partnership, founded in 1956. Landscape is not allowed to be considered as an afterthought, even to the extent of allowing it to dominate architecture, as in their innovative use of roof gardens in the General Accident headquarters near Perth. Climate, together with the use of local materials and skills, are basic considerations and are allied to a strong emphasis on maintaining visual interest of the kind often inspired by traditional styles. Their design for a proposed holiday village next to Dunrobin Castle is an appropriate solution in an historical setting, with good use being made of existing woodlands (see pp 184–5). The Ardnamurchan Visitor Centre, as shown at the Glasgow Garden Festival, is another example of a modern building suitably designed for the Scottish countryside.

Several of the firms mentioned above practise their art furth of Scotland in the time-honoured tradition of Scots. Likewise, architects from other countries have, and are, making contributions to the built environment of Scotland. A recent example of this counter-invasion is the high-tech factory designed by the English architect Richard Rogers for Linn Products of Eaglesham (see jacket), which received an RIBA National Award in 1988. A project still in progress and awaiting implementation is the Maybury Business Park, west of Edinburgh, designed by the American architect Richard Meier in association with the Scottish firms of Campbell & Arnott and Ian White Associates (see p 186–7). Here the designers have evoked the principles of Craig's plan for Edinburgh's New Town in a manner appropriate for its time and place.

LANDSCAPE DESIGN AND PLANNING

While the preceding sections of this chapter describe the developing role of architects in shaping the built environment, two other disciplines – landscape architecture and planning – are also playing an increasingly important part in shaping tomorrow's heritage.

The first Scot to style himself as both a landscape architect and a town planner was Sir Patrick Geddes (1854–1932), using the title of landscape architect in correspondence with the Carnegie Dunfermline Trust in 1907. A biologist by training and educator by inclination, Geddes conducted a life-long campaign for the better integration of the built and natural environment. Very conscious of the contribution by British designers of the past, a visit to Harvard in 1899 made him aware of the major involvement by landscape architects in the planning of cities like Boston and New York. As the father of landscape architecture, Frederick Law Olmsted had submitted his 'greensward plan' for Central Park as early as 1858, the

House at Cramond by
Morris & Steedman, 1957
*(Photo: W. J. Toomey, © The
Architects' Journal)*

House in East Kilbride by
Morris and Steedman, 1965

American Society of Landscape Architects was founded in the year of Geddes' visit and the first university course in the subject was introduced at Harvard in 1900. Observing these events fired Geddes' enthusiasm for the establishment of an environmental design profession in Britain and in 1914 he was a founding member of the Town Planning Institute, along with Thomas Mawson (1861–1933), who had also entered the Dunfermline competition in 1903, and who failed in his bid to have the new Institute called 'The Society of Landscape Architects' on the American model.

Although Mawson was elected an early president of the Town Planning Institute, he soon became disenchanted with the neglect of landscape design by the new professional body and campaigned hard for the subject to be taught as a separate discipline. When the Institute of Landscape Architects was established in 1929 he was invited to be its first president. He was later followed in this office by Brenda Colvin (1897–1981), a prominent practitioner who came under the influence of Gertrude Jekyll as a student and who left her mark by writing the textbook

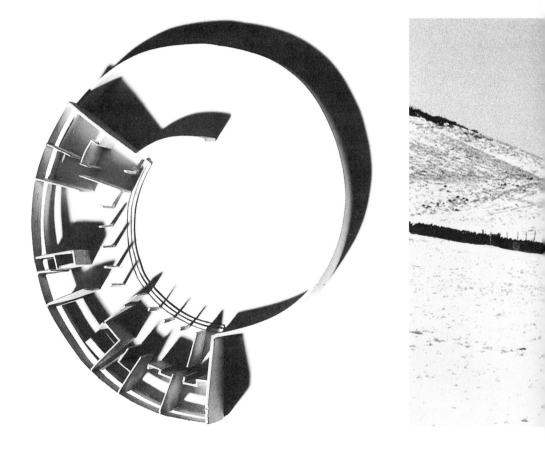

House on the southern slopes of the Pentland Hills near Flotterstone, by Morris & Steedman, 1965. The dwelling and the courtyard are enclosed by a continuous circular wall so that indoor and outdoor spaces are unified into a design solution that is as simple and elegant as the lines of the landscape setting itself

Land and Landscape and by publishing her choice of 60 *Trees for Town and Country*, both in 1947.

The landscape design profession is now well established, Sir Geoffrey Jellicoe and Dame Sylvia Crowe being two distinguished and suitably honoured members. The Institute elected Sir Edwin Lutyens an Honorary Fellow, and its members have included other distinguished names such as Sir Patrick Abercrombie, William Halford and John Dower. Many have combined the professions of architecture, landscape design and town planning, like Sir Geoffrey Jellicoe whose book *The Landscape of Man* has been a source of inspiration for those who believe that history is relevant and that the future lies in working together.

Few Scottish architects of the 1930s would appear to have combined their building work with landscaping, certainly not to the extent of predecessors like Bruce, Adam and Lorimer. Interest among the general public would also seem to have been low, the only seminal work on Scottish gardening from this time being two books, by E. S. Haldane (1934) and by

E. H. M. Cox (1935), both dealing with garden history rather than the work of contemporary designers. The book by Tony Aldous and Brian Clouston for the Golden Jubilee of the Institute (1979) and Harvey and Retting's extracts from the Institute's journal, *Fifty Years of Landscape Design*, provide interesting accounts of progress since that time, but it is a matter of regret that so few published sources exist about work in Scotland, and that distinguished Scottish academics like Frank Clark (1902–71) and Professor David Skinner (1928–89) did not write more about their own work and that of others. The significant contribution made by landscape designers in the new towns, such as by Brenda Colvin at East Kilbride, Sylvia Crowe at Harlow, Frank Clark at Stevenage and Peter Daniel at Livingston, is another story still to be recorded fully.

There was a revival of interest in our landscape heritage in the 1960s, and the Garden History Society was formed in 1965 with Frank Clark as President. Many Scottish books on the subject, by authors such as Professor Tait and Tim Buxbaum, have been published in response to public demand, and the three professions have become more aware of each other's work so that there is now a greater concern to follow a more holistic approach to the environment. The need for future stewardship of historic sites has triggered a response by public bodies, and the Countryside Commission for Scotland and Historic Buildings and Monuments have recently published an inventory of 275 gardens and designed landscapes that are of national importance. Undertaken by Land Use Consultants, this work has highlighted the need to provide proper protection of such sites on the lines of that already given to listed buildings.

The awareness of landscape design and planning was fostered from the 1960s onwards with the establishment of practices by Derek Lovejoy, William Cairns and William Gillespie, who later took on the practice of Dame Sylvia Crowe when she retired. The profession in Scotland came of age, addressing the need to integrate major oil, gas and electricity installations into the landscape, and responding to an ambitious programme of land renewal initiated by the Scottish Development Agency and a major national road-building programme by the Scottish Office. These initiatives generated a need for design and planning skills, and stimulated the establishment of a number of new Scottish practices such as the Turnbull Jeffrey Partnership, James Cunning Young & Partners, the ASH Partnership and Ian White Associates. Some English practices, such as Brian Clouston, Land Use Consultants and Cobhams, have also had a strong presence in Scotland.

Some of these partnerships have carried their professional philosophy forward from their original landscape base to embrace a multidisciplinary approach, like Gillespies who now offer skills across the full spectrum of environmental design and management, including architecture. Their philosophy is founded on the concept of wholeness of place, together with

Modified kit-house at Ebost
on Skye, by Alasdair
Alldridge of Wittets, 1990

Modified kit-house in
St John's Town of Dalry,
by Antony Wolffe

inspiration from Richard England's notion that good design comes from 'voices of the site'. Along with others, the practice has promoted an integrated approach to building and landscape design, highlighted by their work on the master plan for the Glasgow Garden Festival of 1988, which did much to stimulate public interest in the skills and techniques of landscape design. The joint festival stand of Dobbies and the National Trust for Scotland was a particularly interesting essay in traditional Scottish gardening practice (see pp 110–11), designed by James Cunning Young & Partners.

This book frequently alludes to the pitfalls of applying urban solutions in the countryside without the necessary adjustments, but this should not be allowed to overshadow the fact that much can be learned from current practices in urban design and town planning, where greater emphasis is now placed on addressing the whole environment. Writers such as Alexander and Krier advocate that, by planning incremental growth, the city will heal in the timeless way that urban communities grew traditionally – a new way of working that will enrich the urban fabric through greater diversity, and a design approach that is now subscribed to by young Scottish partnerships like Elder & Cannon and Page & Park. In developments for Glasgow's Merchant City, these and other practices have considered the whole of the built environment, from the individual buildings of its internal courtyards, to the external relationship that these have with the street pattern of the wider city. Proper regard for the context of architecture is clearly an issue of common concern to architects, landscape designers and town planners alike. The challenge is to establish a broad front of mutual association across the urban-rural divide to sustain our endeavour in creating a better built environment.

PRINCIPLES OF GOOD PRACTICE

In the words of the Royal Incorporation of Architects in Scotland, it would indeed appear that 'we are looking at the stirrings of a new Scots architecture'. The review of recent trends in this chapter reveals that the 'clean slate' fervour of modernism has subsided to be replaced with a new awareness of the need to accommodate our aspirations within parameters set by the natural environment, and with a recognition that our vision of the future needs to be shaped so that it does not impair the existing cultural heritage. It is encouraging to discover that architects and landscape designers are again working closely together and sharing a language of evocative catch phrases like 'a sense of place', 'spirit of place', 'wholeness of place', 'echoes of the landscape', 'language of site' and 'voices of the site'.

This new language represents a coming together of our timeless traditions, as outlined in the first five chapters, and the modern spirit of innovation attached to the constantly changing technological world of the present, as revealed in this chapter. The work for this book has been undertaken in the belief that a new and enduring heritage can be created, but to achieve this the buildings appearing in the countryside from now on must be of the same high quality as the best from the past. The five concluding principles of good practice provide a guide to this end.

Before starting a project, also remember that a design brief should be prepared and agreed on the lines discussed in Chapter 2. Likewise, remember that good design pays as does quality, and a long-term view should always be taken when making an investment.

Finally, there is the question of aesthetic control of development, which has been the subject of much debate between architects and planners in recent years. The planners have regarded such control as an essential part of regulating the shape of built development in line with agreed planning policies. Architects have resented the interference in matters of aesthetic judgment, and have regarded controls as an unhealthy constraint that stifles creative design. One way to resolve this is through the joint production of design guides, which should set down the ground rules for a given area and for different types of development, and which should have due regard to the whole process of design and development. The principles discussed in this book highlight the need for such guides to address design in a holistic manner embracing both landscape and buildings. Experience of developing large-scale complexes like university campuses and business parks has shown that a master plan for the layout of roads, building plots and landscaping is not sufficient to achieve a built environment of unity and cohesion. For this to happen it is necessary to have a clear vision of what is desired in terms of built form, scale, materials and colour – all of which have to be suitably specified and consistently applied in the manner of our planned towns and villages of the past.

Like all rules, the following principles have exceptions and they should be applied critically. This should be borne in mind when looking at the examples illustrated on these pages. The captions attached to each do not seek to assess the design, and it is left for the reader to judge whether or not the requirements of the following principles have been satisfactorily met. The answer should lie in whether a building is of the same high quality as the landscape itself.

PRINCIPLES OF GOOD PRACTICE

1. Respect the Natural and Cultural Heritage
    - observe the time-honoured response to climate and landform in vernacular architecture
    - respect original style and detailing when converting old buildings, and demolish only as a last resort

2. Locate Development in a Sustainable Manner
    - use locations next to settlements rather than isolated sites
    - work with the climate, contours and scale of the locality

3. Design the Setting to be in Character with the Surroundings
    - treat the whole site as an entity, and design buildings and landscape together
    - use planting and walls to create enclosure, and to tie the buildings into the landscape

4. Built Form and Layout should be Functional and Appropriate
    - use style and scale consistently throughout a site
    - design both internal and external spaces so that their functions and relationships are easily perceived

5. Use a Limited Range of Colours and Materials for Visual Unity
    - use complementary and earth colours for harmony, and bold colours for contrast and emphasis
    - consider the life expectancy and the maintenance of both buildings and landscaping

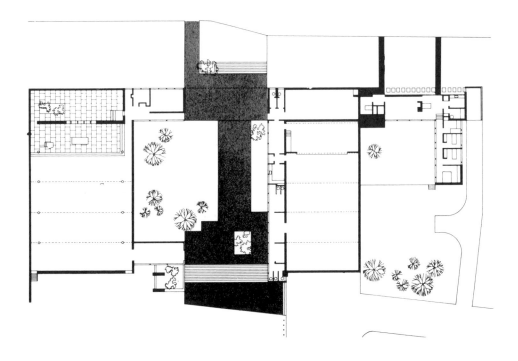

Kildrum Parish Church at
Cumbernauld, by Alan
Reiach and Stuart Renton of
Reiach & Hall, 1962

Gannochy Sports Pavilion at Stirling University, by Alan Reiach and Stuart Renton of Reiach & Hall, 1969. The style is consistent with other university buildings, and the pavilion is stepped into a wooded slope so that the public rooms on the first floor are entered from the car park on the upper part of the site. The changing-rooms below open straight on to the playing fields

Pitlochry Festival Theatre,
by Graham Law of the Law
& Dunbar-Nasmith
Partnership, 1981 (© *A. L.
Hunter Photography*).

OPPOSITE
The use of a model is always
helpful when fitting a large
new building and an
extensive area of car parking
into a sensitive landscape
setting

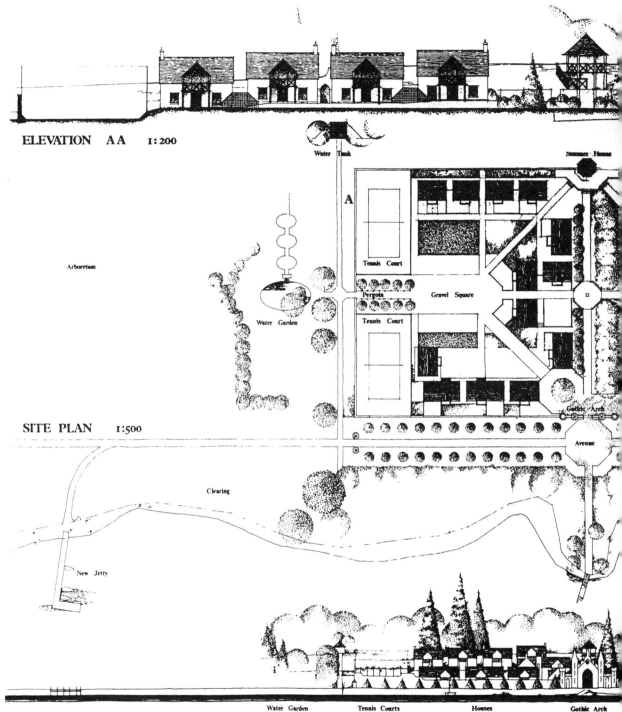

ELEVATION A A 1:200

Water Tank

A

Arboretum

Water Garden

SITE PLAN 1:500

Clearing

New Jetty

Tennis Court

Pergola

Gravel Square

Tennis Court

Summer House

Gothic Arch

Avenue

Water Garden   Tennis Courts   Houses   Gothic Arch

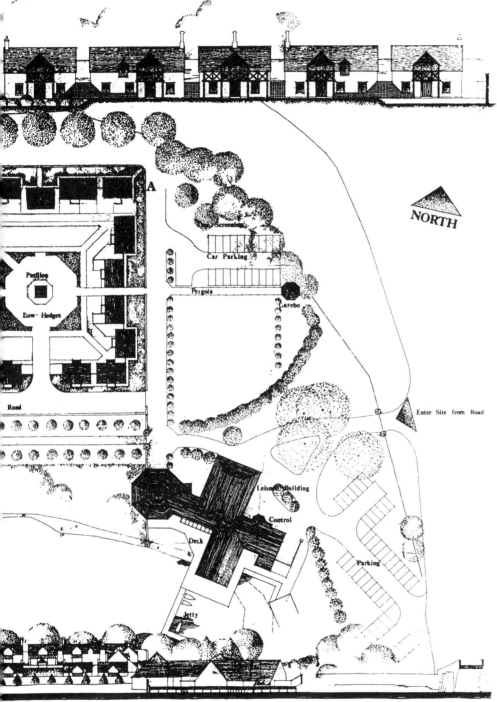

A

NORTH

Road

Pavilion

Bow Hedges

Road

Tree Screening

Car Parking

Pergola

Gazebo

Enter Site from Road

Leisure Building

Control

Deck

Jetty

Parking

Houses

Leisure Building

Bridge to Kenmore

AND OVER LEAF
Master plan for the
Kenmore Club on Loch Tay
in Perthshire, by Brian Paul
of the Hurd Rolland
Partnership. Located within
the walled garden of
Taymouth Castle Estates,
the detached time-share
units are arranged in
terraces to form two
courtyards, with access and
lines of movement related to
the main gates and using the
architectural features of a
summer-house and the
pavilion. The architecture is
a successful combination of
modern styling and the
traditional vocabulary of
scale and form, and the
white harl is the same as in
the local village. Mature
trees have been carefully
preserved and new planting
has been designed to echo
the original garden
atmosphere of the site

Residential units at
Kenmore

The waterside building at
Kenmore, housing the
swimming pool, games
rooms and restaurant
(Drawing: Brian Paul)

Conversion and extension
of traditional farm steading
at Easter Coldrain, near
Kinross, to form hotel and
housing. Architecture and
landscape design by
Gillespies, 1991

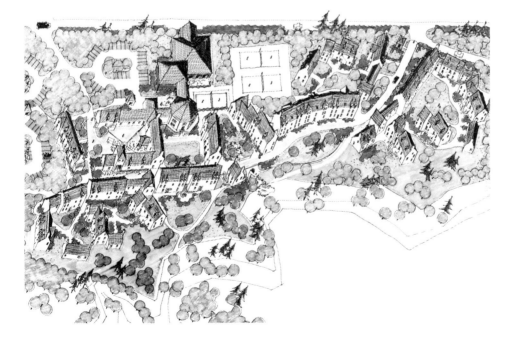

The winning submission for a holiday village, still to be built, in the grounds of Dunrobin Castle in Argyll by Angus Macdonald and Ian Lowden of the Parr Partnership, 1986. The layout of the 150 residential units and ancillary facilities features a traditional high street flanked by a series of courtyards. The architecture is domestic in scale and traditional in styling with a white harled finish. Existing trees are retained, and new planting is designed to complement the spatial structure and soften the visual impact of built development

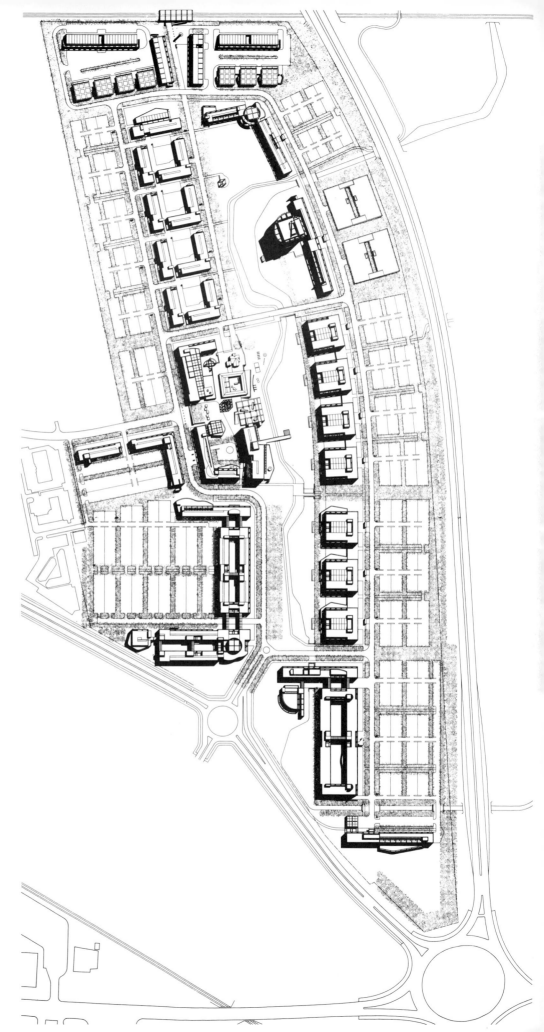

Master plan for 'Edinburgh Park' at Maybury on the western city bypass, by Richard Meier jointly with Campbell & Arnott and Ian White Associates, 1990. The plan draws its inspiration from the site and the urban form of the central city, with the buildings laid out in two terraces facing on to a central green space through which runs a small lake drawn from the Gogar Burn. Planting around the flanking parking lots will define these external spaces and link them to the built form in a manner reminiscent of the gardens in the New Town of the inner city, also echoing the pattern of fields and hedgerows in the surrounding countryside. The real test of the plan will be whether individual developers are required to adhere to the design guidelines, which have been set to ensure that order and unity are achieved in the final product (© *Richard Meier & Partners Architects*)

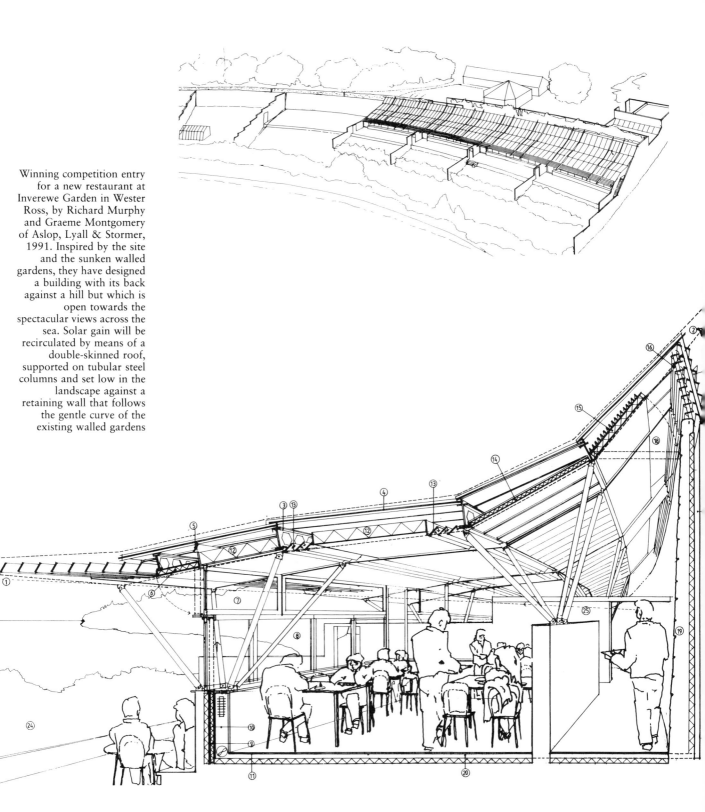

Winning competition entry for a new restaurant at Inverewe Garden in Wester Ross, by Richard Murphy and Graeme Montgomery of Aslop, Lyall & Stormer, 1991. Inspired by the site and the sunken walled gardens, they have designed a building with its back against a hill but which is open towards the spectacular views across the sea. Solar gain will be recirculated by means of a double-skinned roof, supported on tubular steel columns and set low in the landscape against a retaining wall that follows the gentle curve of the existing walled gardens

INDEX

Note: page numbers in *italic* refer to illustrations

Selected Bibliography

ALDOUS, T. & CLOUSTON, B., *Landscape By Design*, Heinemann, 1979

ALEXANDER, C. et al, *A Pattern Language*, Oxford UP, 1977

ALEXANDER, C., *The Timeless Way of Building*, Oxford UP, 1979

ALEXANDER, C. et al, *A New Theory of Urban Design*, Oxford UP, 1987

AYLWARD, G. & TURNBULL, M., *Visual Analysis: the Development and Use of Visual Descriptions*, in *Design Methods and Theories*, Vol 12, No 2 (April–June), 1978

BAKER, G. & GUBLER, J., *Le Corbusier: Early Works by Charles-Edouard Jeanneret-Gris*, Academy Editions (Architectural Monographs 12), 1987

BLACKIE, *Villa and Cottage Architecture*, Blackie & Son, 1876

BOARDMAN, P., *The Worlds of Patrick Geddes*, Routledge & Kegan Paul, 1978

BUILDING RESEARCH ESTABLISHMENT, *Climate and Site Development*, Digest No 350, Parts 1–3, BRE, Department of the Environment, 1990

BURBRIDGE, B. & YOUNG, F., *The Royal Botanic Garden Edinburgh Book of the Scottish Garden*, Mowbray House, 1989

BUXBAUM, T., *Scottish Garden Building: From Food to Folly*, Mainstream, 1989

CHARLES, Prince of Wales, *A Vision of Britain: A Personal View of Architecture*, Doubleday, 1989

COLVIN, B., *Land and Landscape*, John Murray, 1970 (1st Ed. 1947)

COLVIN, B., *Trees for Town and Country*, Lund Humphries, 1965 (1st Ed. 1947)

COUNTRYSIDE COMMISSION FOR SCOTLAND, *Gardens and Designed Landscapes: An Owners' Guide to Planning their Management and Conservation*, CCS, 1989

COUNTRYSIDE COMMISSION FOR SCOTLAND, *An Inventory of Gardens and Designed Landscapes in Scotland*, Vols 1–5, CCS and SDD Historic Buildings and Monuments, 1987

COUNTRYSIDE COMMISSION FOR SCOTLAND, *Lavatories in the Countryside: A Design Guide*, CCS, 1983

COUNTRYSIDE COMMISSION FOR SCOTLAND, *Providing for Children's Play in the Countryside*, CCS, 1986

COX, E. H. M., *A History of Gardening in Scotland*, Chatto & Windus, 1935

CROWE, S., *Tomorrow's Landscape*, The Architectural Press, 1963

CROWE, S., *Garden Design*, Packard, 1981

DE GRANDIS, L., *Theory and Use of Colour*, Blandford, 1986

DEPARTMENT OF THE ENVIRONMENT, *Time for Design – Monitoring the Initiative*, HMSO, 1990

FENTON, A., *The Island Blackhouse*, HMSO, 1978

FENTON, A. & WALKER, B., *The Rural Architecture of Scotland*, John Donald, 1981

FORESTRY COMMISSION, *Forest Landscape Design Guidelines*, Forestry Commission, 1989

HALDANE, E. S., *Scots Gardens in Olden Times (1200–1800)*, Alexander Maclehose, 1934

HARVEY, S. & RETTING, S. (Eds), *Fifty Years of Landscape Design*, The Landscape Press, 1985

HAYTHORNTHWAITE, G., *Space for a New Society in the Countryside*, letter in Journal of the Royal Town Planning Institute, Vol 76, No 38 (28 September), 1990

HOWARD, E., *Garden Cities of Tomorrow*, Faber & Faber (reprint), 1965

HOWARTH, T., *Charles Rennie Mackintosh and the Modern Movement*, Routledge, 1990

HUSSEY, C., *The Work of Sir Robert Lorimer*, Country Life, 1931

JELLICOE, G. & S., *The Landscape of Man*, Thames & Hudson, 1975

JENCKS, C., *The Language of Post-Modern Architecture*, Academy Editions, 1977

JOHNSTON, E., *The Tin Tradition*, in the *Journal of the Royal Institute of British Architects*, Vol 88, No 5 (May), 1981

KRIER, L., *The Reconstruction of Vernacular Buildings and Classical Architecture*, in the *Architects' Journal*, Vol

180, No 37 (12 September), 1984
KRIER, R., *Urban Space*, Academy Edition, 1979
LAND USE CONSULTANTS, *A Study of Gardens and Designed Landscapes in Scotland*, CCS, 1983
LAW, G., *Greek Thomson*, in *The Architectural Review*, Vol 115, No 689, May 1954
LISNEY, A. & FIELDHOUSE, K., *Landscape Design Guide*, Gower, 1990
LUCAS, O. W. R., *The Design of Forest Landscapes*, Oxford UP, 1991
LYNCH, K., *Site Planning*, MIT Press, 2nd Ed., 1962
McKEAN, C., *The Scottish Thirties*, Scottish Academic Press, 1987
McKEAN, C., *Architectural Contributions to Scottish Society since 1840*, Royal Incorporation of Architects in Scotland, 1990
McWILLIAM, C., *Scottish Townscape*, Collins, 1975
MARLOWE, O. C., *Outdoor Design: A Handbook for the Architect and Planner*, Crosby Lockwood Staples, 1977
NAISMITH, R. J., *Buildings of the Scottish Countryside*, Gollancz, 1985
PEVSNER, N., *The Sources of Modern Architecture and Design*, Thames & Hudson, 1968
PRIZEMAN, J., *Your House: The Outside View*, Hutchinson, 1975
PROPERTY SERVICES AGENCY, *Energy Saving Through Landscape Planning*, Vol 1: The Background; Vol 3: The Contribution of Shelter Planting; Vol 4: Existing Housing; Vol 6: A Study of the Urban Fringe, PSA, 1988
REIACH, A. & HURD, R., *Building Scotland: Past and Future*, Saltire Society, 1944
REID, J., *The Scots Gardener*, Mainstream, 1988 (1st Ed. 1683)
RITCHIE, G. & A., *Scotland – Archaeology and Early History*, Thames & Hudson, 1985
ROBERTSON, P. (Ed.), *Charles Rennie Mackintosh: The Architectural Papers*, White Cockade Publishing, 1990
ROYAL INCORPORATION OF ARCHITECTS IN SCOTLAND, *The Architecture of the Renaissance*, RIAS, 1990
ROYAL INCORPORATION OF ARCHITECTS IN SCOTLAND, *Scottish Architecture in the 1980s*, RIAS, 1987
SAVAGE, P., *Lorimer and the Edinburgh Craft Designers*, Paul Harris, 1980
SCOTTISH OFFICE, *Siting and Design of New Housing in the Countryside*, (Planning Advice Note 36), HMSO, January 1991
SHARP, T., GIBBERD, F. & HOLFORD, W. G., *Design in Town and Village*, HMSO, 1953
SINCLAIR, F., *Scotstyle – 150 Years of Scottish Architecture*, Fitzhenry and Whiteside, 1984
TAIT, A. A., *The Landscape Garden in Scotland 1735–1835*, EUP, 1980
TRUSCOTT, J., *Private Gardens of Scotland*, Weidenfeld & Nicolson, 1988
TURNER, T. H. D., *Scottish Origins of Landscape Architecture*, in *Landscape Architecture*, Vol 72, No 3 (May), 1982
US DEPARTMENT OF AGRICULTURE, *National Forest Landscape Management*, in *The Visual Management System, Agriculture Handbook*, No 462 (Vol 2, Ch 1), The US Government Printing Office, 1971
WEAVER, SIR L., *Houses and Gardens by Sir Edwin Lutyens, RA*, Country Life, 1925
WEDDLE, A. E., *Landscape Techniques*, Heinemann, 1979
WILLIS, P., *New Architecture in Scotland*, Lund Humphries, 1977
WHITTOW, J. B., *Geology and Scenery in Scotland*, Penguin, 1977
WOLFE, T., *From Bauhaus to Our House*, Jonathan Cape, 1982

ROYAL INCORPORATION OF ARCHITECTS IN SCOTLAND
Local Architectural Guides:

Brogden, W. A., *Aberdeen*, 1986
Burgher, L., *Orkney*, 1991
Finnie, M., *Shetland*, 1990
McKean, C., *Banff and Buchan*, 1990
McKean, C. et al, *Central Glasgow*, 1989
McKean, C., *The Districts of Moray*, 1987
McKean, C., *Edinburgh*, 1982
McKean, C., *Stirling and Trossachs*, 1985
McKean, C. & Walker, D., *Dundee*, 1984
Pride, G. L., *The Kingdom of Fife*, 1990
Swan, A., *Clackmannan*, 1987
Walker, F. A., *The South Clyde Estuary*, 1986